A sampling of Sam . . .

"Insanity is hereditary. You can get it from your children."

"Today they soundproof the school building —in the old days they soundproofed the students."

"All matters should be approached with an open mouth."

"People are still marrying for better or for worse, but not for long."

"The only person who listens to both sides of a husband-and-wife argument is the woman in the next apartment."

YOU CAN SAY THAT AGAIN, SAM!
The Choice Wit and Wisdom of Sam Levenson
is an original POCKET BOOK edition.

Books by Sam Levenson

Everything But Money
In One Era and Out the Other
You Can Say That Again, Sam!:
    The Choice Wit and Wisdom of Sam Levenson

Published by POCKET BOOKS

# You Can Say That Again, Sam!

## THE CHOICE WIT AND WISDOM OF SAM LEVENSON

by

# Sam Levenson

PUBLISHED BY POCKET BOOKS NEW YORK

YOU CAN SAY THAT AGAIN, SAM!

The Choice Wit and Wisdom of Sam Levenson

POCKET BOOK edition published October, 1975

L

This original POCKET BOOK edition is printed from brand-new plates made from newly set, clear, easy-to-read type. POCKET BOOK editions are published by POCKET BOOKS, a division of Simon & Schuster, Inc., 630 Fifth Avenue, New York, N.Y. 10020. Trademarks registered in the United States and other countries.

To
ELIAS MICHAEL

# Acknowledgments

My thanks to my family for both their encouragement and their loving criticism.

To brother Al, especially, for converting pages and pages of scribbling into a manuscript.

To Larry and Sophie Howitt of Seven Hills.

To Barbara Hendra, Publicity Director of POCKET BOOKS who thought a collection of my best could turn out to be not bad.

To Phyllis Grann, Editor in Chief of POCKET BOOKS, who said, "I love it, I love it," and proceeded to improve it.

To Peter Matson and Gypsy da Silva and Charlotte da Silva and Sheree Stawasz and Peter Schwed and Charlotte Greene and Dave Vern and Carole Schwindeller, each of whom helped in some way.

But most of all to the unsung and unpublished but surely not untalented folk humorists whose delightful observations about life are recorded in many of these pages.

# *Foreword*

Through the years people have asked me for a line or a paragraph that they read in my books or heard me use on TV or in live appearances. "If it isn't too much trouble, Mr. Levenson . . . "

No trouble at all. Thanks for asking.

Here you now have a Request Album of the people's favorites. As with an album of music you can go back again and again to the parts you like.

Personally, the parts I like most are those where my voice and the voice of the people harmonize.

—Sam Levenson

P.S. A suggestion. This is the kind of book which can be read aloud. Try it. It carries off like hi-fi.

# Contents

1

*Old Folks . . .*

*. . . know a lot more about being young,
than young folks know about being old.*

～ ～

The bright sayings of little children are just that
—bright, shiny, innocent. The humor of the aged
is even brighter and shinier but not innocent. Their
sly comments about their expanding limitations are
a form of brinkmanship on the brink of eternity.
They are not at all resigned to their ultimate decline
and departure. Instead of following Dylan Thomas's
advice to "rage against the dying of the light," they
accept it, under protest, using humor as a delaying
tactic.

Here are some of the most poignant "Exit Laugh-
ing" lines from the ranks of the eighty to one
hundred year olds:

"What have I got to complain about? I'm a very lucky guy. I've got two teeth left and they are opposite each other."

\*

"My memory is getting worse all the time. First I began to forget faces, then names, then to zip up. Yesterday I forgot to unzip."

\*

"I beg your pardon, does the ringing in my ears annoy you?"

\*

"The reason I get more quiet as I grow older is that I have more to keep quiet about."

\*

"I set out in life to find that pot of gold at the end of the rainbow. Now I'm eighty and all I've got is the pot!"

\*

"I'm not covered by Blue Cross. I'm covered by Red Cross. I'm a disaster."

*

"I'm worth a fortune: I've got silver in my hair, gold in my teeth, stones in my kidneys and gas in my stomach."

*

"I just want to live long enough to be as much of a nuisance to my children as they've been to me."

*

"I hope I'm really sick. I'd hate to feel like this if I'm well."

*

"I've got so many aches and pains that if a new one comes today, it will be at least two weeks before I can worry about it."

*

"My boy, I was sick before you were born."

\*

"This is my last will and testament: I ain't got nothing; I owe everybody; the rest I leave to the poor."

〜 〜

My Uncle Benny is over eighty and a lifelong comic philosopher. He comes up with an abundance of truisms which turn out not to be true but, before you realize it, you've already been nodding your head in agreement:

"If medical science has made so much progress in the last fifty years, how come I felt so much better fifty years ago?"

\*

"So what if your pants are shabby and worn as long as they cover a warm heart."

\*

16

"Half the people like to work and the other half don't, or maybe it's the other way 'round."

*

"Lucky are the mothers and fathers who have no children."

*

"Enjoy yourself now. Remember, you'll be dead the rest of your life."

*

"Why should we worry about the future? What did the future ever do for us?

∽ ∽

If doubt is the beginning of wisdom, my own mother had a method of imparting doubt by throwing us short, provocative questions that required a deep and often agonizing evaluation of our souls and our goals. This was not lie detection, but truth detection. She never waited for the answers, because they were not for *her* but for *ourselves*.

17

You *need* it or you *want* it?

\*

And if everybody is doing it, so?

\*

And no answer is not an answer?

\*

When is enough already?

\*

Maybe it's better not to ask?

\*

When will you be a man already?

∽ ∽

*At what point do you become an old-timer?*

*You already* are *if you can remember*:

When a bureau was a piece of furniture.

When doctors made house calls.

When castor oil was the wonder drug.

When dope was what they called a less-than-bright youngster.

When any little boy could create his own rainbow by wee-weeing into the sunlight (the primitive form of streaking).

When you used to listen to the ocean roaring inside a large snail shell.

When you could buy something for five or ten cents in the five-and-ten-cent store.

When on cold nights you wrapped a hot brick (or an oven lid) in a towel and put it in bed at your feet.

When the cream at the top of the milk bottle froze and rose a couple of inches out of the bottle. (When milk had cream.)

When kids used to rub wood shavings into their hair and "make like Shirley Temple."

19

When you used to weave a baseball out of rubber bands, and cover it in black electrical tape.

When you used to collect fireflies in a drinking glass, cover it with cheesecloth and stay up at night to watch the fireworks.

When you sat and watched horseflies trying to take off from a landing field of flypaper.

When you dipped pens into inkwells.

*And*—

You could convert ash-can covers into Roman shields, oatmeal boxes into telephones, bottle tops into checkers, broomsticks into baseball bats, discarded mattresses into trampolines, umbrella ribs into bows and arrows, candlesticks into trumpets, orange crates into store counters, peanut shells into earrings, hatboxes into drums, clothespins into pistols, and lumps of sugar into dice.

You also qualify if you can remember resharpening old razor blades by honing them against the inside of a drinking glass, or making a racing car out of a wooden box, a plank and abandoned baby-carriage wheels.

And playing games that required only one player, games that were I.Q.-less and scoreless, but not pointless or joyless—games like looking at clouds to see faces, castles, animals, angels and God; or closing your eyes and holding your breath in front of a mirror to see how you would look if you were dead; or bird-watching (lie on the fire escape and let the birds watch *you*); or staring straight ahead, wide-eyed, just to watch the eye fluid wandering about the pupils of your eyes; or filling in all the *o*'s and making *t*'s out of *i*'s in books and newspapers; or using milk to write yourself secret messages on white paper; or licking a broken tooth in your mouth until you went into a hypnotic trance.

❧ ❧

As you reach your second childhood, you will come finally to live in places where there are no little children to watch at joyous play, places where you will be advised by young experts on aging to give up silly fun for sensible hobbies, like molding clay. (Dust thou art, to dust returnest.)

❧ ❧

I remember when anybody called "Grandma" was a little old lady with grey hair and gold-rimmed glasses who wore a shawl and sat on a rocking chair and rocked and rocked and rocked and rocked. The contemporary grandma is just a little bit different. She goes shopping in cowboy pants, plays tennis in shorts, captains the bowling team and goes belly-dancing on Tuesdays. To put it bluntly—Grandma is off her rocker. Gentlemen who used to help little old ladies cross the street now follow them.

∽ ∽

There is no greater love in all the world than the love of grandparents for grandchildren. As has been said: a genius is a stupid kid with very happy grandparents.

Grandparents are easy to identify:

If you see a man stretched out on a rug with a three year old sitting on his head nailing it into the rug and the man with his dying breath is gasping, "Look how nice he holds that hammer"—that's a grandpa.

If little Albert Einstein is sawing a leg off the dining-room table and there is a little lady standing nearby saying, "Let him, let him, he's playing"—that's a grandma.

There should be a law requiring married couples to become grandparents before they be permitted to become parents.

Babies are so much better off in the hands of older people who value life so much more.

Any kid who has been raised by grandparents

would never want to live with young, impatient,
irritable, cranky parents.

∽ ∾

One grandchild's art project in school was a
drawing of his grandma with a written tribute under
it.

*This is a grandma.*
*When grandmas get old, their hair gets red.*
*At night, they take off their teeth and gums.*
*They talk to God—like when they take off their*
*shoes at night, they cry a little and say, "Thank*
*God."*
*Everybody should try to have a grandma, espe-*
*cially if you don't have television.*
*Most important is: they stop your mother from*
*killing you.*

∽ ∾

23

2

# *Insanity Is*
## *Hereditary . . .*

*. . . you can get it from your children.*

◇ ◇

No mother should be ashamed to admit that the joys of motherhood start when the kids are either asleep or well married. Among the great numbers of people who have volunteered to go to the moon are several thousand young mothers who have offered either themselves or their children. The height of parental maturity is, of course, to learn to live with your child *as he is*—even if he is just like *you*.

If I were a member of the cloth—any of the major cloths, Catholic, Protestant or Jewish—and I were marrying a couple, I would tell the young man to step aside. Then I would turn to the bride and ask her to speak the vows which (like it or not) she will have to uphold in her marriage.

"My dear young bride, repeat slowly after me: I promise to love, honor and cherish and let the kid out, let the dog in, let the dog out, let the kid in, put the kid on the potty, wipe the kid, wipe the floor, take an aspirin, answer the doorbell, let the plumber in, let the kid out, let the plumber out, let the kid in, let the burglar in, let the kid out, take a Darvon, talk to myself, talk to God, light the oven, put in the chicken, scream at the kid, scream at the doorbell, scream at the Girl Scout cookie vendor, pull out the cremated chicken, mop the floor, take a Miltown, wipe the kid, wipe the blood from my slashed wrists . . . and look like Cleopatra when *he* comes home at night."

Then if she still wants to embark on family life, O.K., but there are a few other matters she should be prepared for. Tell her now that these are the things a normal child will do, not because his mommy said or did anything to crush his little spirit, but because he's normal:

He will bite people, throw hairbrushes into toilet bowls, stick marbles and buttons into his nose, swallow keys and safety pins, fall out of windows, stick pinkies into electrical outlets, cry and hold his breath for twenty minutes while turning blue, lock himself into bathrooms, finger-paint walls with io- dine, disappear from his crib at night, walk out into the street naked, put pennies between the keys of the piano. . . .

∽ ∽

The mother should know that she will have to read a bedtime story to the kid, the very same bedtime story, every night for the first four years of his life, and he won't let her skip a word (even after he's been asleep for two hours). He will make secret doo-doos in secret corners, which no one will ever be able to find. If he is toilet-trained, he will use a full roll of toilet paper every time he goes, whether he goes or not. He will invariably pull off his galoshes with his shoes still in them. He will tie his shoelaces into knots a sailor couldn't open. He will drink one quart of milk per day and spill three. He will prefer to eat food that he finds on the floor rather than on the table. He will lose fourteen handknit left-hand mittens by the time he's six years old.

Furthermore, he will catch colds that will last about three weeks; the cough will linger from two to three years. His tonsils will finally have to be removed; he will then cough louder and clearer for two years after that. He will demand a tankful of tropical fish that will die in three days; the tank will stand there empty for eleven years. He will also require a twenty-seven-dollar Cub Scout uniform which he will wear to one meeting and then drop out.

∽ ∽

The future mother should be forewarned that kids no longer *grow* by years. They *develop*. We grew by years; they grow by stages. The child has got to go through all the normal stages. (He will survive all the stages; the mother may not.)

During the first normal stage he spits on people. Don't get upset, mother. This is normal development. The second stage he lies. (My father would have called him a "dirty liar." He was wrong.) This child "has imagination." It's a stage. All the world's a stage. Then he goes through the dirty-word stage which, according to the best authorities, is considered not only normal but necessary.

My father used to wipe out the three stages with one of two methods: either backhand or forehand. (For him that was normal. It was a stage he never outgrew.)

I knew psychiatric terms like "sympathetic pain" by the time I was three years old. If my father hit my brother, I cried—because I knew I was next.

〜 〜

Some psychological terms every mother should know:

1. *High-I.Q. Child:* A kid who says dirty words earlier than other kids.

2. *Autosuggestion:* The parental compulsion to jump into an auto (or in front of) and get away from it all.

3. *Hallucinations:* Seeing visions of kids without running noses.

4. *Self-expression:* In a child, any act which cannot be explained rationally.

5. *Sex Maniac:* A husband who wants more children.

6. *Siblings:* Children of the same parents, each of whom is perfectly sane until they get together.

(My mother settled sibling warfare by arbitration. She would bring the two conflicting parties together and explain to them that violent behavior is a sin against God and man. Then, when she thought they understood, she would bang their heads together to leave a lasting impression on their minds.)

〰 〰

Child punishment current American-style runs somewhat along these lines:

About six-fifteen P.M., the mother gets very dramatic, turns to the child and says, "Go to your own room." He's got a television set there; he's got his own refrigerator; he's got a train set that goes through the other people's apartment and back again; they send his dinner in to him, leave him for the evening with an eighteen-year-old baby sitter and he's being punished. His father didn't live like that on his honeymoon!

〰 〰

It *is* advisable that the kid have his own room. Even my mother knew that. We had our own room —all eight of us in our own one room. Each kid had his own closet too: a nail on the back of the door. First one up in the morning was the best-dressed for the day.

There is also a new rule which forbids parents from walking into their kid's room without knocking. The kid walks around with the Bill of Rights in his diaper and knows what he is entitled to. He's been advised by his four-year-old civil-rights lawyer (the kid next door) that his lease entitles him to privacy.

We didn't even have privacy in the bathroom. We had to sing. The minute you stopped singing the next kid was in. If he was very polite, he might knock on the door and call in, "Hey, Sammy, you through singing?"

"No. Give me one more chorus."

If you stayed too long, notes came under the door: "Hurry up." "You're not alone in the world." "Get moving."

There *were* locks on the bathroom door. I remember the hook-and-eye lock. But who had a hook and an eye? If you had a hook, you didn't have an eye. If you had an eye, you didn't have a hook. Or, you had a slide bolt that used to slide into nothing.

⌒ ⌒

"Kids today have more freedom than we had." That's what everybody says. It doesn't look that way to me. They call it T.L.C., Tender Loving Care. To me it looks more like protective custody.

Nowadays when the mother takes the baby out for a stroll in his carriage, he is strapped around the waist, under the armpits, over the shoulders and into a crash helmet buckled under his chin. If the carriage went off a cliff, this kid wouldn't get a scratch.

In his high chair (modeled after the electric chair) his feet are pinned down, two belts criss-cross his chest, and his hands are manacled to prevent him from doing violence to himself.

His playpen is a padded cell in which he is tethered by ropes with bells on them to warn of a possible break. Built into one wall is an abacus on which the prisoner can count off the days of his confinement. Food is placed in the pen in an unbreakable cup which he bangs against the bars to get attention. His "Yah, Yah" can be taken to mean what it usually does in prison movies: "I'm not eatin' this slop. I'm gettin' outa here."

Baby's gotta have shoes. He's only four months old, doesn't even need stockings; he ain't going nowhere, but he's gotta have shoes. Not ordinary shoes, God forbid. Corrective shoes! There are no more children with straight feet. We used to walk straight; they all walk crooked. No more shoe stores. Every store is a clinic. Every shoe salesman is a professor with glasses. They X-ray the kid's feet. (He hasn't got bones yet.) They ask him, "Do they fit?" What should he tell them? He can't talk yet. And he doesn't have to walk. They give him a little balloon and he floats out of the place.

When the first snowfall of winter comes, the mother has got to get him dressed to go out and enjoy the snow that God sent for *him* and for nobody else but *him*.

So they get him dressed as no American in history was ever dressed before: seven sets of leggings, eight sweaters, then a snowsuit with a zipper that travels over the body, over the head, over the ears. Only his nose is sticking out. Stiff as a board. He can't move. He just stands there and waits for further orders. They pick him up under both arms, carry him out into the street and stick a shovel in his hand.

In front of each house is one *him* with a shovel, slowly freezing into position. They try to make contact with each other before rigor mortis sets in: "Hey, Alfred, you wanna play?"

"Sure, I wanna play. Come and bend me, so I'll play."

This is the moment that the *him* in the seven zipped-up leggings and the eight zipped-up sweaters has got to make a wee-wee! The race is on between his mother and Mother Nature:

"Hold it! Hold it, I'll murder you, hold it! Eleven times today already. Wait till the other suit dries at least. Hold it!"

No use. Just as you're down to the last zip—too late!

∽ ∽

Every kid must, of course, be provided with plenty of toys. Open the closet door in his room and thirty thousand dollars' worth of rarely used toys will slide out onto the floor. Where did they come from? We bought them because we read a book that says a child should have interests and hobbies, and it's our responsibility as the parents to jack up his I.Q. So we took all our savings out of the bank and turned it into toys—educational, of course.

All I want to know is why he walks around saying, "I got nothing to do today. Take me someplace." My father used to say, "I'll take him. I won't bring him back, but I'll take him."

One of the best-selling educational toys is a stick on a stand with rings which the child is supposed to glide down the stick. The mother, father and two sets of grandparents sit in the corner watching and waiting for the great day when he will be able to slip that ring over the stick. "He made it! He made it! He's got an I.Q.! He's intelligent!" (When I was a kid I did the same thing with bagels over my index finger. They thought I was a dumb kid.)

∽ ∽

What was more educational or more beautiful than the maternal affection little girls bestowed upon their rags dolls, those wonderful practice babies which they hugged to pieces, dragged about in shoe boxes, slept with, sang to and loved? In the child's imagination that rag doll talked, sang, cried. The battery-powered doll of today walks better than its owner. It also sings, winks, drinks, talks, wets, gags, hiccups, recites, swallows safety pins and develops diaper rash. Sometimes the wires get crossed and, instead of singing, it wets. The time will come when this little doll, like its owner, is going to come up with a pre-taped: "I got nothing to do. Take me someplace."

∽ ∽

The richer the family, the less the kids play. Rich kids play by appointment. Two mothers call each other on the phone and make plans. "Yes. We'll have them meet." And they meet after school.

"Hello, Richard, I'm Gregory."

"Hello, Gregory."

"Hello, Richard."

"Did you bring a toy, Gregory?"

"Yes. I brought a toy, Richard."

"What is the toy?"

"It is a ball."

"A ball? Where are the instructions?"

I used to run out of the house to hear eighty kids yell, "You're 'It.'" I didn't even know what game they were playing. I used to start running; I'd find out later what game they were playing. I can tell you something else. I used to *win*, and I didn't know what game I was playing.

～ ～

Rich or poor, every kid has either run away from home or threatened to. Most of them get as far as the doorway and give their parents a last chance to call them back. I have heard:

"I'm gonna run away from home and I'm gonna run so far it'll cost you fourteen dollars to send me a postcard."

\*

"I'm not coming back. Remember that! I'm not coming back even for religious holidays."

\*

"I'm gonna join the Marines or the Foreign Legion or maybe I'll even go to the moon. I would

37

leave right now but, lucky for you, it's snowing
outside."

∾ ∾

Some kids do run away in style. This is what the
police found on a fugitive from one wealthy suburb:

*His transistor radio.*
*Two dozen rock-and-roll records.*
*A space helmet.*
*A picture of his dog.*
*A roll of pink toilet tissue.*
*His electric guitar.*
*A half-chewed-up little blue blanket.*
*His father's credit card.*

∾ ∾

3

# "When I Need
## Your Opinion . . .

*. . . I'll give it to you,"* Papa always said.

〜〜

He also helped me to overcome the usual identity crisis of adolescence by regularly asking me, "Who do you think you are, anyhow?"

Papa was not a pal to his children, nor did I expect him to be one. He was my father. Not only that. He had been a perfect kid. You can't beat that. In fact, the only perfect kid I ever heard of was my father when he was a kid. By the time I got to know him he was already an active member of U.P.A.—Unafraid Parents of America.

(This was all before children became the new ruling class, the Kindergarchy—government of the kids, by the kids, for the kids, with the parents retained as loyal servants, permitted to answer the phone, take phone messages and, on special occasions, to eat with the children.)

My generation is the most obedient generation of all time. We got the best training for it. First we obeyed our parents; now we obey our children.

When I was a kid I had to do whatever my father wanted me to do. Now I have to do whatever my kids want me to do. All I want to know is when am I going to do what I want to do?

I hear rumors that an organization is being created to help parents addicted to palism. It is called Palcoholics Anonymous. Its purpose is to protect weak heads of families. When the temptation becomes too great, a palcoholic can dial MOuse 1-8000, and two men will come and remove him to some safe place. The sponsor of this organization was a father who, before he realized how far he had strayed into palcoholism, found himself driving his kid around for trick or treat.

❧ ❧

According to social-service agencies, a good home is one which provides love, acceptance, high moral standards, good parental example, decent food, clothing, shelter, spiritual guidance, discipline, common enterprises, a place to bring friends and respect for authority. Any child, rich or poor, who lives in such a home may be considered a "lucky kid." I was a lucky kid.

❧ ❧

In my parents' home these were the House Rules:

*Respect is to be shown all elders.*

*There is no such thing as a petty crime. Little offenses can lead to big ones. Practice makes perfect.*

*The menu at mealtime offers two choices: take it or leave it.*

*The management reserves the right to screen your friends.*

*When the sun sets you come home. Growing things don't flourish in the dark.*

*You have to earn everything: grades, money, trust.*

*You* can *be a hero in your own home. Try it. Anyone who brings honor to this house is.*

∽ ∽

Family life in my parents' home was based upon a cosmic order: Papa was the sun; Mama, the moon; and we kids, minor satellites. We received light, energy and direction from one another. You could count on the sun and the moon to keep us in our proper places. If you got out of orbit, you were out of order.

∽ ∽

Our parents weren't always right, but they were clear—sometimes loud and clear. They figured that if they didn't teach us, someone else would. "Go outside. See what Sammy is doing and tell him to stop!" Their position was consistently maintained on what *they* believed was proper concerning dating, marriage, smoking, drinking, cosmetics, manners, hours, money, clothing, teachers, books, lying, cheating, sex, movies, jobs, homework, punishment, obedience, friends, cleanliness, language, truancy, study. . . . Somehow through it all, perhaps *because* of it all, I felt loved.

Parents will forcibly pin down a child when he is getting a shot of penicillin "for his own good," but, when strength is required for a moral shot in the rear, they become powerless.

It takes both courage and foresight to say as my father did: "I don't care what you think of me this minute; I am concerned with what you will think of me twenty years from now." It takes even greater courage to say: "Better that the children should cry than the parents." Ask any juvenile-court judge.

❧ ❧

On the other hand, if you want to be a good shnook-type of parent, here are half a dozen ways to be one, and guarantee yourself a rotten kid:

*Shnooks' Law I:*

Never force him to do anything he doesn't feel like doing. He can force you, but you can't force him.

*Shnooks' Law II:*

Never raise your voice to him. Always remain calm, even when they're taking you away.

*Shnooks' Law III:*

Tell him all about his rights, but never mention his responsibilities or your rights.

*Shnooks' Law IV:*

Make sure he knows all the four-letter words except: Duty, Home, Help, Care, Earn, Save, Give, Work, Love.

*Shnooks' Law V:*

Never say to him: "If you want to improve the human race, suppose you start with you?"

*Shnooks' Law VI:*

Never mention the word "gratitude," especially when he's borrowing the car or collecting his allowance. It may embarrass him.

∽ ∽

Gratitude is high on the list of my personal priorities. I was bred on it. "Thanks, Ma, thanks for the violin lessons, for the shoes, for the education, thanks, thanks, thanks. . . ."

If insisting on gratitude from our children seems like an excessive demand, maybe we can call it recognition, acknowledgment, or even social justice.

Since the young want us to "tell it like it is," here, in their language, is a love letter to a sophomore from the parent body, "told like it is":

*Darling Soph:*

*You were born of a parental love-in. Right off we got hooked on you, and we didn't need LSD to get turned on. You were our thing, and we built our establishment around you. We held daily demonstrations of our loyalty. We resisted all injustices toward you. We practiced nonviolence against you even under provocation. We held all-night sleep-ins at your bedside when you were sick, and there was pot, much pot, which we carried to and from; and when the fever went up to 104, we held a pray-in to overcome. We gave you free love, a wall-to-wall carpeted pad of your own and the best education we could (or could not) afford. We never freaked out when the going was rough. Now you are ready to remake the world for the better. We are with you. Just one request, if we may. When the brotherhood of man is established, could you maybe make the membership broad enough to include motherhood and fatherhood? We want in. We want in! We, too, belong to now, and we cherish our now dearly, because we can't count on as much of it as*

*you can. Toss us a* flower *now and then—preferably*
*now!*

> *Lovingly yours,*
> *The Committee for Peace, Love*
> *and Amnesty for Parents*

∽ ∽

# 4

# School Days Are the Best Days of Your Life . . .

*. . . provided your children are old enough to go.*

∽ ∽

In the old days they sent you off to school at age six and picked you up after graduation at age fourteen. In the interim you were supposed to sit still, listen and learn. Today they soundproof the school building; at that time they soundproofed us.

The three most frightening words a student could hear were: "Bring Your Mother." It was the equivalent of a death warrant. You pleaded, you cried, you invented heartrending excuses. "My mother can't come. She's sick, she can't climb stairs, she's dying, I'm an orphan, I live all by myself. Bring my father? He died four years before I was born, he can't come, he works in Alaska, he comes home only on Saturdays. What did I do? Tell me! I'll never do it again. I never did it before so I'll never do it again.

Today's mother is an integral part of the school

scene. In some schools there are more mothers present than kids. If the mother is absent, the kid has to write a note of explanation. "Please excuse my mother for being absent. My mother's mother is sick."

The modern mother is much more mobile than mine was.

The following "ad" appeared in the Lost-and-Found column of a P.T.A. newspaper.

*Lost, one wife. Last seen headed to or from: School-Board Meeting, or Garden-Club Meeting, or Knitting-Club Meeting, or Class-Size Rally, or Boy Scout Rally, or P.T.A. Envelope Stuffing, or Sisterhood Smorgasbord, or City Council Protest, or Peace Pray-In, or Save the Library Sit-In, or Save the Bridge Walkover, or Save the Bay Swim-In, or Clean the Streets Bendover, or Pave the Pavement Parade.*

*Come Home!*

*Am afraid to stay in the house all by myself.*

*Your loving husband*

*P.S. Our marriage license may have expired.*

∾ ∾

Students, too, are mobile. They don't "go" to school. They are driven there, either by their parents or by a bus driver. The roads are jammed with road scholars.

Education is now portal to portal. You've seen them, the kids with the green faces on the yellow buses. For these kids someday car exhaust will bring back memories of school days.

You can't let a kid walk. He might get hit by a snowflake and have a concussion. So the mother drives the child to the corner and keeps his body warm in the car until she can deposit him into the warm bus. By the time he gets to college he will need a course in remedial walking.

It had to happen. For nine months before he was born his mother carried him. After that he lay around in his crib for a year contentedly sucking on a bottle. From there he went to the playpen where, for two years, he sat around contemplating his navel. Then he went to a tricycle until the school bus came for him. At sixteen he got his own car. On his wedding day they carried him down the aisle, still wearing his baby shoes. He had never had a chance to use them.

Paradoxical but true. The school spends $20,000 for a bus so the kids don't have to walk, and then spends $200,000 for a gymnasium so the kids can get exercise.

Many days when the students arrive at school they don't even enter the building. They just change buses and leave for a field trip. My daughter, Emily, went on more field trips in her first year of school than the average farmer does in a lifetime. Her class visited a bakery, a stable, a glue factory, a printing shop, a shoemaker, a carpenter shop, a

53

little old wine maker. . . . In my time, I passed all of these and more as I walked to school every morning.

Some of Emily's answers to the question "What did you learn in school today?" proved a shock to her parents:

"We didn't learn nothing today. The bus broke down."

or:

"We didn't learn nothing today. The bus driver broke down."

But, surprisingly, she learned to read; and what she learned to read in those first years she can still read, better than anyone I know—bus signs.

∽ ∽

Spelling now comes under the heading of creative arts. Any kid who can't spell a word more than one way lacks originality. Any teacher who insists on spelling the same word the same way all the time is probably a bigot. A kid who omits some letters from a word is entitled to partial credit. If he adds extra letters, he's entitled to extra credit. To compel a kid to write clearly may reveal the fact that he can't spell. This invades his constitutional protection against self-incrimination. Nor can a teacher say to a kid: "When in doubt, consult a dictionary." In the first place, these kids are never in doubt; in the second place, how can you consult a dictionary if you can't spell?

It is more practical to start by teaching them to print rather than to write. This is a skill which can be used later on for ransom notes, graffiti and picket signs. Besides, you can't expect legible handwriting from a kid who's doing his homework while puking in a moving vehicle.

∽∾

Show and Tell is one of the current methods for getting children to express themselves in ways other than writing. You don't even have to have *something to say*. You just have to *say something*. Anything! All matters should be approached with an open mouth. Silence is not golden. It is a symptom of a potentially dangerous inclination toward introversion.

There is one teacher who, on the first day of school, sends each of her students home with the following note:

*We start Show and Tell tomorrow. If you promise not to believe everything your child says happens in class, I promise not to believe everything he says happens at home.*

I know of at least one very enlightened nursery school that has managed to include sex education under the heading of "Show and Tell." To make it all very natural they maintain co-ed bathrooms. This gives little girls the right to stand up for their rights and little boys the right to sit down for theirs.

∽ ∽

A poor report card used to mean that the child was lazy, inattentive, bad, not very bright, or just like his father. A bad report card now means that the teacher is lazy, inattentive, bad, not very bright, or just like the principal.

These days if a teacher has to flunk a kid, she will have to answer to the mother. A bad mark is the teacher's fault. "I don't want to make trouble for you, Mrs. Jones, but my mother says if I don't get a better report card next time, somebody's gonna get killed."

So, some teachers resort to self-defensive euphemisms to avoid sending the kid home with the naked truth:

Richard is a very relaxed child. (Naked truth: he sleeps all day.)

Linda participates fully in class discussions. (Naked truth: she never closes her big mouth.)

He's emotionally immature for first grade. (Naked truth: let him bring his own mop.)

Contributes nicely to group singing by helpful listening. (Naked truth: he's been warned not even to hum.)

But, there still are heroic teachers who will lay it on the line:

I'm giving Arthur a zero. He doesn't deserve a zero but that's the lowest mark I'm allowed to give.

\*

Time will pass, but not Richard.

\*

Not only is your Donald the worst-behaved kid in the class, but he has a perfect attendance record.

∽ ∽

Children have always been richly creative in their explanations for a poor grade:

"That's no zero, Pop. The teacher ran out of stars, so she gave me a moon."

\*

"That *F* in spelling? That's for Fenominal."

∾ ∾

In my fifteen years as a schoolteacher, I learned that some of the smartest (perhaps even the wisest) answers come from the simplest minds. These answers may not be *correct,* but they are still *right:*

Q. What do we call the last teeth to appear in the mouth?
A. False.

The finest distinction between heredity and environment I ever heard came from an eight-year-old boy who put it this way:

If a baby looks like his father, that's heredity. If he looks like some other man, that's environment.

∾ ∾

I was raised in the time of the times tables. We used to recite times tables for company.

58

"Hey, Sammy, recite the two times table for Uncle Louie."

I'd get up and say: "Two times two is four, two times three is six, two times four is eight." Once you'd mastered the two times table, you went on to the three times table and the four times table and the five times table. "Sammy, get up on the chair and recite the eight times table. . . . Did you hear that kid?" (Applause.)

A nine times tabler was about ready for marriage!

Unfortunately, different teachers were divided into different schools of tables. As a result, some kids said: "Two times two *is* four." Some kids said: "Two times two *makes* four." Other kids said: "Two times two *equals* four." Still other kids said: "Two times two *gives* four." (A new teacher could mean trouble.)

There was also something we knew as the "gozinters." Two gozinter four, four gozinter eight, eight gozinter sixteen. And there were the "summerwitches": the summerwitch is four, the summerwitch is eight. There were also eagles: two plus two eagles four.

And there was such carrying on about the carryovers. Carry over the number one in your mind. Now put back the number one from your mind. Now (if you haven't lost your mind) cross out the carryover from your mind.

And then there was a big to-do about the remains. Bring down the remains, carry over the remains, take away the remains, put back the remains. ((I thought I was being trained to be a mortician.)

And there were moral implications. Some fractions were proper and behaved themselves while some were improper. I never really found out what it was about them that was improper. Even my very proper parents couldn't tell me.

The schools said that our arithmetic was practical. In fact, the book was called *Practical Arithmetic.*

I vaguely remember some of those practical problems. They are no clearer to me now than then:

Mary is twice as old as John. Three years ago Mary was three times as old as John was then. Ten years from now John will be two times as old as Mary would have been if John were seven times older than his Uncle Julius.

Q. How old is John's Uncle Julius?
Method: Let x equal Mary
        Let x + y equal Mary + John
        Let x − y equal Mary − John.
        Now carry Mary over to the John.
        Carry Mary and John to two places
        and remove their decimals.

Here's a practical problem for a kid in a tenement:

*A boat is going upstream at twenty knots . . .* I knew only that knots were used to hold up my pants.

*The stream is going downstream at forty knots . . .*

I was lost before they got to the question. I had never seen a stream. I knew only that I was up the creek, with seven brothers and one sister all in the same boat paddling upstream against poverty.

Another practical problem:

*If you had thirty-two dollars to spend . . .*

Ans.: Stop! If I had thirty-two dollars to spend, my mother would've turned me over to the police. Or even better than that, if I had thirty-two dollars to spend, I would hire someone to do my homework.

The teacher said I wasn't good in arithmetic. Sorry, Dear Teacher, but that was not the whole story. It wasn't that I didn't *understand* the arithmetic; I just didn't *believe* it.

In my arithmetic books they dealt in quantities I had never heard of: bushels of tomatoes, crates of eggs, sacks of grain, bunches of bananas, carloads of watermelons, truckloads of potatoes, gallons of vinegar, barrels of flour, hogheads, tons, acres, pecks, shiploads. In our home we dealt with somewhat smaller quantities like a bite, a lick, a leftover, a crumb.

YOU CAN SAY THAT AGAIN, SAM!

*John's mother bought a twenty-pound roast for three dollars . . .*

Just a minute!

My mother could never afford to buy a twenty-pound roast at any price and, believe me, there would be no "remainders."

*John has fifty dollars and would like to buy a new suit, a new coat and a new hat . . .*

Ans.: "So would Sam, Teacher."

〜 〜

We no longer can help our children with their homework. ("Help your father or he'll be up all night with your homework again.") Even if the parent gets the right answer, he's still wrong. ("That's not the way the teacher does it.")

Our children are not learning our arithmetic in school anymore. They are now learning mathematics, the new mathematics. They do not know about my gozinters or summerwitches. They work with sets, subsets, concepts, properties, numeration, pairs, facts, members; in fact, they can add anything but numbers.

One advantage of the new math is that you don't have to get the exact answer so long as you understand what you are doing. When we sent Emily to the grocery and she forgot to bring back the change, I asked her, "Where's the change?" She said, "Theoretically, there was no change." (Somehow she always asked for her allowance in the old arithmetic.)

There is also something called "estimates." For example: If a dog has four legs and the kid says three, he has the nearest estimate. Hurrah for the kid! For the dog it's tough, but for the kid, hurrah!

I heard a kid in an Orthodox Jewish school go for the supreme estimate. "Two plus two, God willing, is four."

❧ ❧

If we want to make education practical I should like to suggest *A Practical Math Primer for Our Times:*

1. Eight-year-old Richard watches 238 murders per week on TV.
   Q. At what point will he develop a lifelong immunity to bloodshed?

2. The cost of living goes up 20 percent each year.
   Q. How long will the average American have to live before he can afford to?

3. TV transmitters are on the average 500 feet higher than church steeples.

Q. How much higher does a man have to look up to TV than to Heaven?

4. If America's former enemies are now America's friends, and America's former friends are now America's enemies . . .
Q. How many enemies should we make now so we can have some friends later?

5. Last year five million children were sent to summer camp for an average of two weeks.
Q. 1. How many came back with both sneakers?
Q. 2. Is a handmade wallet really worth six hundred bucks?

6. If one car makes one teen-ager happy and two cars will make him even happier . . .
Q. How many would make him happiest? (Give answer in accidents per week.)

7. It is stated that only 10 percent of marijuana smokers go on to heavy drugs, but 90 percent of heavy drug users start on marijuana.
Q. Who should get off the pot?

8. A schoolteacher gets $5.00 an hour. The TV repairman gets $12.50.
Q. How much time and money did the repairman save by not going to college?

∽ ∽

All jobs today are given professional titles so that all occupations will sound executive. Hardly anyone wants to be known as a workingman. We are not far from the day when job classifications will read as follows:

| JOB | TITLE |
|---|---|
| Undertaker............ | Outdoor Excavation and Layout Engineer |
| Garbage Man.......... | Transporter of Surplus Commodities |
| Pickpocket........... | Self-Employed Public Fund Raiser |
| Washroom Attendant.... | Director of Seating Arrangements |
| Laundryman........... | White-Collar Worker |

∾ ∾

More and more of our children are going to college. From their occasional letters to home we can get a clue to their personal, moral and intellectual growth:

*Dear Mom:*

*I want to thank you for letting me live away from home. It has taught me to get along on my*

65

own, to make decisions and to look after myself.
I lost my vitamin pills. What shall I do?

> Your loving daughter,
> Mary

\*

Dear Dad:

Don't be surprised when you see me. My hair is
down to my shoulders now. Everybody is doing it.
It is not really a revolt against authority or anything
like that. It's just that I want to think for myself,
like everybody else around here.

> Your son,
> Lewis

\*

Dear Dad:

This electronic world is destroying man's soul. I
wrote a folk song about it which I play on my electric guitar.

> Your loving daughter,
> Julia

\*

Dear Dad:

I've just finished a battery of electronic aptitude

tests. *The machine says my greatest aptitude lies in any business in which my father holds an influential position.*

*Philip*

*

Dear Dad:

*My roommate here at Harvard is the son of one of the professors. He's very unhappy because he can't go to an out-of-town college.*

Your son,
Harry

*

Dear Mom:

*It's only fair to tell you that I have already done it. All I want is your consent.*

Your loving daughter,
Mildred

*

Dear Mom:

*There is a lot of kissing and necking going on around here and I don't like to be left out of it. Is it O.K. with you if I remove the braces from my teeth?*

Your loving daughter,
Teresa

*

*Dear Mom:*

*This is a very open-minded college. You can do anything you please as long as you leave the door open.*

> *Your loving daughter,*
> *Alice*

\*

*Dear Mom:*

*You've been wonderful to me throughout college —my own apartment with George and summers with George in Europe. When George and I get married, may we live at home with you for a while?*

> *Your loving daughter,*
> *Anna*

\*

*Dear Mom:*

*I have volunteered for an experiment on the influence of promiscuity on personality. Don't panic. I will not use my right name.*

> *Your loving daughter,*
> *Gertrude*

\*

*Dear Mom and Dad:*

*I am now at home in the arts and at home in the sciences and at home in literature. I shall not be at home for the holidays.*

> *Happy New Year,*
> *Frances*

\*

*Dear Dad:*

*I have come to the decision that it is time for me to stand on my own two feet. I shall call collect Sunday night to explain.*

> *Frederick*

\*

*Dear Dad:*

*I hate everybody here. Everybody here hates me. I won't be home Friday. We are having a love-in.*

> *Your son,*
> *Arthur*

\*

Dear Dad:

   *If you think you can afford it, I would like to take a Ph.D. in poverty.*

                     *Your loving son,*
                     *Hank*

\*

Dear Mom:

   *Our course on twentieth-century living stresses contraception, venereal disease, drug addiction, homosexuality and other modern problems. Next semester we shall discuss postgraduate problems.*

                     *Your loving daughter,*
                     *Susan*

\*

Dear Dad:

   *I have like decided to major like in English. Beautiful prose like turns me on. I wanna wail like them other way-out cats.*

                     *Are you with me, Daddy Baby?*
                     *Your son,*
                     *Melville*

                   ∾ ∾

5

*About Intellectual*

*Giants . . .*

*. . . and ethical dwarfs.*

❧ ❧

I believe that each newborn child arrives on earth with a message to deliver to mankind. Clenched in his little fist is some particle of yet unrevealed truth, some missing clue, which may solve the enigma of man's destiny. He has a limited amount of time to fulfill his mission and he will never get a second chance—nor will we. He may be our last hope.

In a world where all things appear to have a meaning, what is *his* meaning? We who are older and presumably wiser must find the key to unlock the secret he carries within himself. The lock cannot be forced. Our mission is to exercise the kind of loving care which will prompt the child to open his fist and offer up his truth, his individuality, the irreducible atom of his self. We must provide the kind of environment in which the child will joyfully deliver his message through complete self-ful-fillment.

All children are special. There is hardly a child without some gift worth developing, and each child's contribution should be celebrated with much rejoicing.

We are not really all created equal. We are created equally precious and equally different. The difference is sacred. We differ temperamentally, environmentally, physically, psychologically, intellectually, economically. Some of us are slow, some fast, some placid, some nervous, some energetic. We have the equal right to make of our individuality a thing of splendor.

❤ ❤

There are many political and social movements whose earnest purpose is to save the world. My personal commitment is to the philosophy expressed in Sanhedrin 4:5 which says that whoever saves one life will be credited in Heaven with having saved the whole world.

I did not learn any of this in my teacher-training courses. Nor did I find it in the teaching curriculum. It came from home, or very close to it.

❤ ❤

When I became a teacher I looked forward to the opportunity of transmitting great moral values to my students.

While waiting for my first class to arrive, I wrote myself a prayer:

*Lord, give me the wisdom to discover in each child his spark of divinity, the gift which You have given him, and through love and guidance nurture this spark into a glowing flame.*

*Let me not favor any one child at the expense of others. Let all be equally worthy of my devotion without regard to their intelligence, their religion, their race or their wealth.*

*Let me teach a love of America, by keeping ever alive her commitment to the greatest good for the greatest number, in the belief that these children are Your greatest good and Your greatest number. . . .*

*Lord, help! They're coming into the room right now, all forty-two of them. Any small miracle will be greatly appreciated.*

*Amen.*

Each day as I faced my classes I remembered my Bar Mitzvah day, the day I came into my ethical inheritance. Before a packed congregation I was presented with the rights of manhood. I had to accept these rights in a speech written not by me, nor by my elders, but by tradition. I stood up and in a changing voice read aloud: "I now have the right to do right, to do justice, to do good, to serve humanity, to help the needy, to heal the sick, to look after my country, to strive for peace, to seek after truth, to fight oppression, to liberate all mankind from bondage. . . ." As I read on I realized that I had been taken. What rights? These rights were really obligations, commitments, responsibilities. I began to catch on. My rights and obligations not only became inseparable but, together, formed a moral mandate. What tradition was telling me was that responsibilities exercised by all guaranteed the rights of all.

◇ ◇

I left the teaching profession after many years with the sad realization that the public-school system was not rooted in a worthwhile all-embracing philosophy of education. We taught spelling, reading, writing, science, mathematics, English and foreign languages, but made no attempt to instill in our pupils great values and great moral criteria on which to structure their lives.

The English word "education" comes from the Latin *educere* ("to lead out of or from"). The assumption is that education leads out of or from ignorance. The system did not ask "toward what?"

The world has had its fill of matriculated, graduated, even decorated men who have led masses of people back to barbarism. (I wish there were some way of revoking their diplomas.)

In our current zeal for consciousness-raising we have neglected to raise consciences.

The arithmetical (arithmetic plus ethic) concept of a richer personal life through gaining by sharing, multiplication of happiness by division and subtraction from the larger to add to the smaller, should be written into the day-to-day curricula of our schools.

Our education is heartless. It is more important for the child's first reader to say, "Love, Dick, love" than "Jump, Dick, jump." It is just as easy for a child to learn the word "pity" as it is to learn the word "kitty," "kiss" as "miss," "hug" as "bug."

It is never too early to teach the shaping of emotional swords into plowshares. Is it kind or cruel? Choose the kind. Is it peaceful or violent? Choose the peaceful. Among the living, newborn or aged, there may be the ultimate messenger of peace we have all been waiting for; in committing violence (in any form—hunger, ignorance, racism) upon even the lowliest of men, we may destroy this messenger. Perhaps (God forbid) we have already done so.

❧ ❧

Patriotism has generally been predicated upon dying for your country. Love of country has as much to do with living for it as dying for it. Not just live and let live. That is not patriotic enough. Patriotism should take on the moral imperative to live and *help* live.

As a schoolteacher I would give America a grade of eighty in patriotism. How did I arrive at that figure? We have a population of about two hundred million. Our government admits that some forty million people are living below what we call the American standard. The question is, do we destroy the entire social order and start from scratch, or does the eighty percent take on the responsibility of seeing to it that the other twenty percent joins the mainstream of American life.

The elementary reading texts in our public schools should face the realities of American life, good and bad.

Chapter one (with appropriate pictures) can be:

MY LAND

I picked two easy words to start with—My Land. Now we may begin to read:

*My land.*
*It is my land.*
*It is a free land.*
*It is a good land.*
*It is free.*
*It is good to be free.*

(Hold everything, and you'll see what I'm up to.)

78

Page two: a picture of the American flag.
Text:

## THE FLAG

*My flag.*
*It is a flag.*
*It is my flag.*
*It is a free flag.*
*It is a good flag.*
*It is good to be free.*

The words are simple; the ideas are not. However, I believe that children are capable of understanding great, even difficult ideas when they are properly presented.

Discussion should now be opened for a definition of what "good" means, what "free" means, what "my" means.

The previous reading material can now be done with question marks:

*Is it* my *land?*
*Is it a* good *land?*
*Is it* a free *land?*
*If not,* why not?

Correctives are now in order. Now!

Any young person who feels that America is not free, or not good or not his, should be encouraged to speak up now and give his reasons for believing what he believes. To postpone discussion of our un-resolved national problems leads to anger and finally to bloodshed.

(Children who at the age of eight are still salut-ing the flag with "I pleg an eagle to the nicest state in America" or "with liberty just as far off" or "one nation invisible" are not learning much about pa-triotism.)

I know that it takes a superb teacher to handle this kind of material but we should train superb teachers; we should have superb schools so that our children can become superb citizens. Now, when our children are four, five, six, seven, eight, is the time to talk of freedoms, rights, responsibilities, duties.

The goal is to attain a grade of one hundred per-cent, which means good for all, free for all, but not a free-for-all. Freedom means the right to choose of one's own free will to be somewhat less than free or not free at all on behalf of some other equally precious human value, such as sacrifice ex-ercised freely for the common good.

∽ ∽

6

# There Ain't
## No Hell . . .

## ... vs. the Hell There Ain't!
### Debate This Sunday.

∽ ∽

It is not written anywhere that religion has to be stuffy. Over the years I have gathered from church bulletin boards, newsletters and announcements, some delightful wit and whimsy about man and God:

ASK ABOUT OUR PRAY-AS-YOU-GO PLAN.

COME IN AND HAVE YOUR FAITH LIFTED.

IF YOU HAVE TROUBLES, COME IN AND TELL US ABOUT THEM. IF NOT, COME IN AND TELL US HOW YOU DO IT.

COME IN AND LET US PREPARE YOU FOR YOUR FINALS.

GIVE UP POT FOR LENT.

PRAY UP IN ADVANCE.

WE HOLD SIT-IN DEMONSTRATIONS EVERY SUNDAY MORNING.

WHERE YOU GO IN THE HEREAFTER DEPENDS ON WHAT YOU GO AFTER DOWN HERE.

DAILY SERVICES. COME EARLY IF YOU WANT A BACK SEAT.

*On charity boxes:*

YOU CAN'T TAKE IT WITH YOU, BUT YOU CAN SEND IT ON AHEAD.

DON'T EXPECT A THOUSAND-DOLLAR ANSWER TO A TEN-CENT PRAYER.

GIVE IN ACCORDANCE WITH WHAT YOU REPORTED ON YOUR INCOME TAX.

∽ ∽

I saw a cartoon in a church newsletter which showed two angels sitting on a cloud. One is asking the other: "Tell me the truth, Robert. Do you believe in the heretofore?"

∽ ∽

You've probably seen the drawing done by a Sunday schooler which shows a long, black limousine, a chauffeur in the front with a little stick coming out of his head with a halo on it and, in the back seat, a man and woman dressed in nothing but leaves. Underneath it is the caption: "This is a picture of the Lord driving Adam and Eve out of the Garden of Eden."

❧ ❧

Some kids believe not only that God helps those who help themselves, but that He especially helps those who help themselves by asking Him to help them. These little supplicants usually call up God at bedtime when the rates are lower:

" . . . and, please, Lord, make Stewart stop hitting me. By the way, Lord, I've mentioned this before!"

"And God bless Mommy, Daddy, Aunt Martha, Uncle Stanley, Grandma and Grandpa, but not my brother Steward, because he socked me again today."

"Remember what I asked for last night, dear Lord? Well, it's ditto tonight!"

"Tonight I'm saying a prayer for my baby sister because she's too young to pray. She ain't even hardly toilet-trained yet."

"And if I die before I wake, please call my teacher and tell her I won't be in school tomorrow."

"I'm not praying for anything for myself—just a new bike for my brother that we can both ride."

". . . and I don't want to go to Heaven if my piano teacher is going to be there."

". . . and, dear Lord, please put vitamins in candy instead of in spinach."

"Help me to be a good boy and, if at first You don't succeed, try, try, again."

"God bless my sister, God bless Mommy and God help Daddy."

∽ ∽

Many of our older traditional young people insist that they no longer believe in ritual; yet, like pilgrims, they come barefoot from all corners of the earth for festivals, but they do not call them pilgrimages. They will gather before an illuminated stage in the woods, but do not call it a shrine. They will partake of bread and wine, but do not call it communion. They wear peace medals and love medals, but do not call them sacred medallions. They hold silent vigils, but do not call them retreats. They practice transcendental meditation, but do not call it prayer. They have gurus, but do not call them prophets. They congregate for sit-ins, love-ins and talk-ins, but do not call them congregations. They will not say "Amen," but they do say "Right on!" They have come not to the end but to the beginning of tradition. So many of our late pagans have become early Christians and even earlier Jews.

～ ～

Some of the best statements on the brotherhood of man have in fact come from my brothers and sisters of all ethnic backgrounds:

Some people are so prejudiced they don't even listen to both sides of a phonograph record.

Disliking people requires a reason; loving doesn't.

The difference between a conviction and a prejudice is that you can explain a conviction without getting angry.

For those who can't think, the least you can do is rearrange your prejudices once in a while.

You can't believe everything you hear, but you can repeat it.

God made the earth in a circle so that each one of us would be the same distance from Him.

There is no color difference between a Chinese gentleman and an English gentleman with jaundice —except that the English gentleman doesn't feel so good.

The Women's Liberation movement will be glad to hear little Clarence's rebuttal to the premise that all men are brothers: "No they ain't. Some are sisters."

◇ ◇

As a former teacher I can tell you that if you want to see brotherhood in action, if you want to see sharing, helpfulness, cooperation and togetherness, just watch a bunch of high-school kids taking a final examination. That is the time when there is no question of race, creed or color. There is only one question! "Who's got the answer?"

◇ ◇

Most people want to be brotherly, but find themselves thwarted by personal likes and dislikes. The Scripture is aware of this. That's why it says: "Thou shalt *love* thy neighbor as thyself." It does not say you have to *like* him, nor does it say, "See footnote

1 regarding color, shape of nose, texture of hair, ethnic classification." No exceptions!

❧ ❧

*

I cannot define the word *love*. I cannot say *what* it *is*. I can say only that I know *when* it *ain't*. I can feel its absence in the marrow of my bones: sometimes, as living hostility; at other times, as deathly cold indifference. In the same manner I also know when *soul* ain't, and when *justice* ain't, and when *compassion* ain't and when *brotherhood* ain't.

The fact that I cannot positively define any of these does not stop me from performing the act which may turn *ain't* into *is*. The millennium will begin when all the "ain'ts" shall have become "ises," and all the *ises* shall be for *all*, and it has to start now, with me. Not an I for an I, but an I for an us. "We, the people . . ."

❧ ❧

7

*If You Can Yearn*
*for It . . .*

*. . . you can earn for it.*

∽ ∼

We had a permissive father. He permitted us to work. Moral support was all Papa could afford to give us.

Papa was impressed by a newspaper story reporting that Rin Tin Tin earned over $200,000 a year. "And *we* had to have children," Papa lamented.

"I'd like to go to college," brother Joe said to Papa, and Papa encouraged him: "Somebody's stopping you?"

Often Papa would prod us with, "You know what Lincoln was doing at your age?" We knew what Lincoln was doing at Papa's age, but we knew better than to bring that up.

I learned from experience that if there was something lacking, it might turn up if I went after it, saved up for it, worked for it, but never if I just waited for it. Of course, you had to be lucky, too, although I discovered that the more I hustled the luckier I seemed to get. Besides, most of the happiness was in the pursuit.

As my Uncle Benny used to say, "It's not the sugar that makes the tea sweet, but the stirring."

Papa helped each of us get started on the road to success: "Remember, my son, if you ever need a helping hand, you'll find one at the end of your arm. And remember, too, if you want your dreams to come true, don't sleep.

"You will finally have to do it yourself: free yourself, educate yourself, support yourself."

We were the "undesirables" of our time, the "them" of then. The only way to rise above undesirability, Mama taught us, was not merely to become desirable, but to become indispensable in some trade or profession. "You need to make yourself needed, my son."

❧ ❧

We were also taught that money isn't everything, but the way you spend it may determine everything, so spend it wisely and, if you can't do that, be wise and don't spend it at all, because if you spend it, you won't have it for a rainy day and, since you can't tell how many rainy days there are going to be, don't spend even on rainy days, and also put aside something for cloudy days, drizzles, mists and who knows what.

I was raised to believe that frugality was not just a good habit; it guaranteed a good life. "You may have to do *without* today if you want a tomorrow *with*." A frugal boy would surely become a prosperous man.

A penny saved was not just a penny earned. A penny saved saved a person from the humiliation of dependence upon others. "You can't hold your head high with your hand out."

Today's poor are being lured into participating in the privilege of our opulent society by contributing their last full measure of patriotic prodigality. The pendulum has swung from "Spend what you have left after you save" to "Save what you have left after you spend."

∽ ∽

Mama saved not only money but children.

In school we learned one kind of arithmetic; at home, another. One plus one equals two was fine with our teacher, but not good enough for Mama. She demanded to know one plus one equals two *what*? Mama's was a method of remedial arithmetic aimed at remedying our poverty by judicious spending. It worked something like this: 1 pair of skates = 12 violin lessons. Cancel out the skates and carry over the lessons. She balanced the equations on her scale of priorities and made sure the needle pointed to our future.

95

1 phone call = 1 carfare to a museum
4 movies = 1 shirt
1 bicycle = 10 pairs of eyeglasses
5 ice-cream sodas = 2 pairs of socks

It was a form of reverse budgeting, planning ahead not only for what not to buy but for buying the instead of, which she could not afford not to own. This kind of juggling, borrowing from our desires to meet our needs, forced minuses to become pluses and liabilities to become assets. She knew the world would never examine her books, but it would examine her children. (She had only one set of these.)

～ ～

The penny I saved for a rainy day has come upon bad days. Pennies lie around in desk drawers alongside rusty paper clips and dead rubber bands. They are even scorned by machines: "This machine does not take pennies." Neither do toll bridges, turnstiles or panhandlers. Children give them to their fathers.

The truth is that pennies are hardly worth pinching. The only thing you can still get for a penny is your incorrect weight. "A penny for your thoughts" is now fifty dollars an hour with the psychoanalyst. Penny banks sell for $1.80 and take only dimes. An apple a day costs more than calling the doctor. And if the doctor tells you you're sound as a dollar, you're really in trouble. The way the world is going, the only thing I will have left for a rainy day is my arthritis.

I owed it to myself to do well, but I didn't know I was going to owe it all to Uncle Sam. For being a good boy and working hard I give *him* money.

Now, if I give my Uncle such a generous allowance every year, don't I have the right (like Papa) to ask, "What are you gonna do with the money?" Look, dear Uncle, you try to live on your income, and I'll try to live on mine.

∽ ∽

Here are a few personal messages brave souls have appended to their income-tax returns:

*Gentlemen:*
*Why don't you simplify the form? Just ask:*
*Whadja make? Whadja spend?*
*Whadja got left? Send it in!*

*

I'm telling you guys for the last time! My wife's relatives *are* an organized charity.

*

Sure you call it take-home pay. Tell me, where else can you go with it?

\*

I told you four years ago I'm dead. Stop sending those stupid blanks!

\*

I'm gonna put all my money into taxes. They're sure to go up.

\*

Who said Columbus was an Italian?
He was the first real American.
When he started out, he didn't know where he was going.
When he got here, he didn't know where he was.
When he got back, he didn't know where he'd been.
And he did the whole thing on borrowed money.

∽ ∾

How charity, the helping of the less fortunate, is best exercised for the good and welfare of the individual and society was superbly expressed by a distant relative of mine, Moses Maimonides, who died in Spain in the year 1204. These are his levels of charity:

The first and lowest degree is to give—but with reluctance or regret. This is the gift of the hand but not of the heart.

The second is to give cheerfully but not proportionately to the distress of the suffering.

The third is to give cheerfully and proportionately but not until we are solicited.

The fourth is to give cheerfully, proportionately and even unsolicited; but to put it in the poor man's hand, thereby exciting in him the painful emotion of shame.

The fifth is to give charity in such a way that the distressed may receive the bounty and know their benefactor, without their being known to him. . . .

The sixth, which rises still higher, is to know the objects of our bounty, but remain unknown to them. . . .

The seventh is still more meritorious; namely, to bestow charity in such a way that the benefactor may not know the relieved persons, nor they the name of their benefactor. . . .

The eighth and most meritorious of all is to anticipate charity by preventing poverty; namely, to assist the reduced brother either by a considerable gift or a loan of money, or by teaching him a trade or by putting him in the way of business, so that he may earn an honest livelihood and not be forced to the dreadful alternative of holding up his hand for charity.

✧ ✧

I am the beneficiary of the eighth level. It has left me with a great debt, one which I shall never be able to repay in full. I am forever indebted for the opportunity given me to work, to earn and to pay for what I need.

✧ ✧

**8**

*Ownership Is*
*Relative . . .*

## *. . . the more relatives the less ownership.*

∽ ∽

Our parents were specialists in the resourceful use of resources. They had never heard of ecology. They knew only that if you didn't take care of what you had, you wouldn't have it. The prolongation of life was one way of serving God. Resurrection after death was not in our hands; resurrection before death was. Our theology took care of our ecology.

The maximal use of raw materials is possible only in a home in which ownership is relative. We were taught that the good earth and all the things upon it were only on loan to us and that we had an obligation to divvy up everything with the needy —and who wasn't needy at some time or other?

We lived not only on borrowed time, but on borrowed shoes, sweaters, coats. I wasn't sure I would inherit the earth. I was sure of Mike's pants. And I made sure he took good care of them.

In Mama's home nothing was embroidered "HIS" or "HERS." Mama had embroidered our minds with "It's not his and not hers, it's everybody's; but it would be very nice if you asked may I have it for a while, thank you very much."

"Ma, should I start a fresh towel?" still runs through my mind. When visiting people's homes I cannot bring myself to use one of those nice, clean guest towels. I use either the inside of the shower curtain or the bottom of my host's bathrobe. My hands are clean and so is my conscience. "I didn't start a fresh towel, Ma."

To this day I am haunted by the mottoes on Mama's kitchen walls: "Waste Not, Want Not." "Willful Waste Makes Woeful Want." I stare in sad wonder at what poor as well as rich families leave on the sidewalks these days for the Sanitation Department to cart away. We are being spoiled faster than our possessions. I see lamps, umbrellas, TV sets, playpens, baby carriages, bicycles, tables and refrigerators cut down in the prime of life, prematurely junked along with some still good, hardly used values.

We are now in the throes of a throwaway syndrome. "Get a new one"—a new suit, a new car, a new building, a new city, a new country, a new world, a new human race. This one is bent, soiled, cracked, worn, old, dirty, dull. Hurry! Hurry! We must not run out of things to waste. Waste and want . . . wanton wasting.

We have been educated to buy. We shall now

have to be *re*-educated to use and *re*use, *re*new, *re*vive, *re*claim, *re*pair, *re*prieve.

We have the best-fed garbage cans in the world, filled to overflowing with food that has been stabbed, cut, tasted and rejected. We throw away the skin, the fat, the gristle, the bone.

∽ ∽

No one ever had to urge us to eat. (With our appetites, if you had put sugar on a fly it would have tasted like a huckleberry.) They tried to distract us. One brother would say, "Look who came in." I would turn my head, and my meatballs were gone. They told me I ate them, and I believed them.

"There is no such thing as bad food," Mama used to say, "there are only spoiled children."

"Ma, I'm hungry."

"Have a little bread and butter."

"I don't like bread and butter."

"If you don't like bread and butter, you're not hungry. The children in China would be glad to have it." (Also: Armenia, Russia, Alaska, India, Africa, Asia, Rumania . . .)

"Liver for the cat" was a common ruse. Everybody knew it, including the butcher.

"Mr. Butcher, the liver you threw into the order yesterday for the cat was not fresh."

105

"Did it make the cat sick?"

"Sick! He couldn't go to school for two days."

∽ ∾

My elegant brother Mike made Mama's left-overs sound gourmetish by giving them French names: hamburger accumulé, liver réclamé, ragout prolongé, beef retourné, onion refraîché, salmon rejuvenée, eggs renaissance, pâté continué, soupe toujours and caviar jamais. Garlic, cabbage, peppers and radishes repeated by themselves. (Papa had trouble finding something to bless in Mama's food which he had not already blessed on previous occasions.)

I have seen kids these days take bites out of an ice-cream cone. We never did that. We started by licking. After you had licked the ball of ice cream down to the rim of the cone, you inserted the mouth of the cone into your mouth and blew into it. This sent the now-softened cream down into the lower half of the cone. You then bit the small tip at the lower end, making a tiny hole. Now you did not blow, but sucked, a tiny drop at a time, holding it under your tongue without swallowing for as long as possible. When the cone and the ice cream gave out, you went back to licking your fingers, all ten, one at a time, slowly.

∽ ∾

9

# The Other Men in
# Mama's Life . . .

. . . were the groceryman, the laundryman, the chicken man, the seltzer man, the fruit man, the candy-store man, the fish-man, the herring man, the iceman, the pickle man, the egg man, the drugstore man, the shoe-store man, the milkman. Each was a man (like Papa) with a wife (like Mama), children (like us) and trouble (like ours).

Mr. Man ran the kind of place to which any mama could safely send any kid alone.

"My mudder says she wants meat for the cat. She says to make it lean. My fodder don't like fat."

"My mudder says she wants for five cents animal crackers. She says, if you don't mind, you should please take out the pigs.

∽ ∼

All the years that have passed have not dissipated the memory of the aroma of fresh-baked bread. I would often go to the bakery on my own, not to buy, but to browse.

At the grocer's, the piquant fragrance of fresh-ground coffee would make me shudder. I would turn my back toward people lest they see, perhaps laugh at, this poor boy's shameless indulgence in such rich sensuality.

Garlic garlands hung from nails on the walls along with braided necklaces of violet onions and oriental figs strung on hemp. The spigots of dark, soggy barrels dripped oil and vinegar, which was sold "loose." Beans, barley, sugar, peas, salt, rice, pepper, cloves, allspice, cinnamon sticks, thyme and poppy seeds lay exposed in open sacks. I walked around not only smelling them but visualizing the ports of call from which they had come, a multiple sense experience that today might be described as smellavision.

～～

The supermarket is too much for me. I am easily overwhelmed by overabundance. More or larger is not necessarily better. I do not believe that "super" equals "superior." Even the superlative may be superfluous.

We have come a long way from the outhouse when bathroom tissue is offered in enough varieties to reflect the décor and/or the accessories of that special place and/or the personality of the person making personal use thereof. Yellow? Blue? Chartreuse? Plaid? Perfumed? Rose? Gardenia? Soft? Facial? Squeezable? Single-strength? Double-strength? Heavy-duty?

∽ ∽

In addition to tourist information, the supermarket must provide other services.

Station yourself next to the front desk and you will overhear lines like:

"For cereals take Route 17, then make a sharp right at the tomatoes."

*

"Sorry, I don't know the brand name but I can hum a few bars of the commercial."

*

"Where can I get some, if you'll pardon the expression, bathroom stationery?"

*

111

"But it says here on the package: 'Return Unused Portion of the Product and Your Money Will Be Refunded.'"

"That's right. Just return the unused portion of the product, and we'll return the unused portion of your money."

*

"Where do you complain about the Complaint Department?"

*

"Is it too late to exchange last week's liver for next month's *Reader's Digest?*"

*

"Did anyone turn in a little brown bag with a urine specimen?"

*

*At the check-out counter:*

"These are two for fifteen, lady; go back and get another."

"And lose my place in line? I'd rather pay the difference."

\*

"You say that last week this item was a penny less? You'll have to talk to the manager, lady."
"Where's the manager?"
"He's not with us anymore."

\*

"This box of cookies is empty, lady."
"I know. I had to eat them to keep alive while waiting on line."

∾∾

Supermarkets deal with so many people each day that there are bound to be accidents. Many stores run first-aid stations. Some injuries are serious; others can be handled by a den mother in residence.

\*

"I was hit by a runaway shopping cart, corner of Catchup and Sardines."

\*

"Some jolly green giant just stepped on my foot."

\*

"There's been a tuna-fish landslide. Some woman is trapped under 2,000 cans."

\*

"My kid fell into the ice-cream freezer and he's getting Popsicled stiff."

\*

"A man is caught in the OUT door and his eggs are getting scrambled."

\*

"They marked down the beef and there's a stampede in the Meat Department."

∽ ∽

Some supermarkets provide a one-hour detention camp where they keep kids busy singing educational songs like: "Little Boy Blue, Come Blow Your Horn, The Sheep's in Aisle Seven, and Nine Is for Corn." There are still enough Hansels and Gretels either abandoned or accidentally separated from one another or from their mothers to keep the Lost-Children's Desk busy all day:

"Did you see a mother without a kid that looks like me?"

\*

"Any lost mothers turned in lately?"

\*

"I forgot my name and address. All I know is my zip code."

\*

"Why am I standing here hollering 'Mary'? What should I holler—'Mother'? The place is full of them."

\*

Lost kids who cry a lot are given ice cream and then put on one of the electric ponies to shake until they are either homogenized or claimed.

∽ ∽

There was a time when hunger was associated with poverty. This is no longer true. I have seen wealthy families reduced to near starvation as they wait for their dinner to thaw. (Very often a defrosted lamb chop may turn out to be a banana fritter.)

Perhaps because we are not handling the present with much success, science is teaching us to freeze life and store it for the future. We are about to do to humans what we have already done to chickens. Freeze them. "Don't call us; we'll call you."

∽ ∽

Mama bought a fresh, whole chicken. Her daughter's chicken has been eviscerated, dismembered, neatly disjointed, frozen, and all its organs sorted out and filed into plastic see-through bags. The young housewife has been spared the bloody ordeal of chicken surgery. Chicken can now be bought in parts. Anyone can create his own version of a chicken out of a do-it-yourself chicken kit. Put together two heads, one eye, three breasts, and four feet; add a mandolin, and you've got yourself an original poultry Picasso.

∽ ∽

The new shopping requires a knowledge of the new math. The relationship between the size of the

116

box and the size of its contents is established by a mathematical formula worked out on the manufacturer's slide rule: The size of the box is four times the size of the tube it contains; the tube itself is four times the size of its contents; and the price is four times the size of the value. This is based on the adage: You can't fool all the people all the time; but most of the people most of the time is close enough.

An interesting test was recently made by a store manager. He put boxes of soap chips on the shelf in four sizes: Regular, Giant, Economy and Full. The Economy size was sold out immediately.

∽ ∾

Getting out of the supermarket is much more difficult than getting in. It is somewhat like leaving a foreign country. "What do you have to declare?" There are two lanes marked LOCAL, two marked EXPRESS, one TEN ITEMS OR LESS and seven lanes marked THIS LANE CLOSED. Any lane may be closed at the discretion of the customs officer if said lane should become dangerously overcrowded by one person.

∽ ∾

10

# "How Did They Live
## Years Ago . . .

*. . . without all these electronic devices?"*

*The answer, of course, is self-evident. They all died.*

*Someday our grandchildren are going to ask about us: "How did they live years ago with all those conveniences?" I can tell them right now. "Kids, it wasn't easy!"*

*You see, we had been trained by our parents only for living with people, since people were about the only possessions we had. We had to retrain ourselves for living with people-free paraphernalia.*

∽∽

Not all of the "latest things" have made me happy.

I wish I could invent some way of uninventing: escalators which threaten to amputate my toes; unmanned elevators which order me around ("Step to the back, please"); tissue boxes which force me to take no more than one tissue at a time; phone-message machines which advise me in a thirty-second pre-recorded speech that I will have ten seconds to talk when I hear the beep in five seconds; dry cleaners' code numbers stapled onto the zipper of my pants; battery-operated lazy Susan coffin lowerers; pay-toilets (especially when you are without time or dime); and, above all, printed questionnaires which have to be filled out with crosses, checks and circles.

How well I remember all the years I labored to improve my penmanship via the Palmer Method, a system of cultivating beautiful circles and oblique strokes guaranteed to give my handwriting the elegance of a papal secretary. I remember the hours I was kept after school to get the curse out of my cursive writing. As the sun went down I sat there rounding and slanting on pages of lined, yellow paper to the rhythm of the teacher's song: "Round, round and round we go, elbow off the ta-able! Wrist off the ta-able! Up and down! Push, pull! *Round*-er! *Round*-er!"

And I cannot forget the vows I made to my teachers never to forget correct spelling, grammar, syntax, syllabification, punctuation and capitalization, never to end my sentences with prepositions, and to keep my participles from dangling—all "so that someday you may be able to express your thoughts more fully, Samuel."

Those rectangular boxes into which I must now fit the body of my thoughts look to me like small, white coffins. Don't box me in. Not yet. I'm still alive. . . .

*They* have spaces that need to be filled. *I* have needs that must be filled. I need to tell the whole story, not just the little part that fits the little hole. A mind repeatedly forced into blanks may finally become one.

Man, endowed with that incredible computer known as the human brain, has used it to invent an electronic brain that will protect him from the dangers of personal involvement. Electronic impulses prevent man from acting on human impulses. Except for the fact that the information we store in the machine may be prejudiced or obsolete, the machine is assumed to be more objective and, therefore, more honest than man. It cannot be sentimental. (Tears rust the components.) Its mistakes, too, are superhuman. It would take fifty people working day and night for two hundred years to make the same mistake an electronic computer can make in two seconds.

❧ ❧

Since our faith in computers is almost total, I should like to offer a resolution regarding a new use for them:

Whereas, the key words of our age are speed, automation and electronics, and whereas, the key words of our age are also violence and moral chaos,

and whereas, man is apparently willing to abide by the absolute judgment of the computer,

be it therefore resolved that there be fed into the computer the Ten Commandments, the Sermon on the Mount, the Bill of Rights and the Declaration of the Rights of Man,

and, be it also resolved that when in doubt about the just application of human knowledge, private or public, man be required to press a button marked MORAL DECISION,

and, be it also resolved that the decision of the computer be irrevocable and binding upon all men.

❧ ❧

I would also like to ask the computer a personal question: is it possible that what counts most in life cannot be counted at all?

❧ ❧

Man's days are numbered; and modern man, like his ancestors, will die when his number comes up.

The tombstones of national heroes may rate a few heartfelt words power-chiseled into the marble:

*Here, subtracted from our total, lies one who amounted to much, respected alike by both numerator and denominator, a magnetic figure, dynamic in his impulses to the nth degree, who will be mourned by all manpower.*

The grave marker of the mere mortal, however, will provide all the vital statistics necessary to preserve his memory:

HERE
TO THE BEST OF
OUR KNOWLEDGE
LIES
00017642/63/.04
HATCHED 1910
MATCHED 1930
DISPATCHED 1975

∽ ∽

I am not ungrateful for America's practical concern with emancipating us from manual slavery by creating machines, but somehow this goal has run into trouble. We, the people, are now working for the machines that are supposed to be working for us.

∽ ∽

My mother could have gotten along fine without the invention of the wheel. With eight kids and Papa to look after, she couldn't go anywhere anyhow. My wife has two children and lots of places to go, and she has the wheels to get her there. However, she can't leave the house because a man is coming to do for her the one thing she can no longer do for herself—repair the machines that are supposed to do everything for her.

∽ ∽

You can still get a part for a dead chicken, but a part for a dead machine is almost impossible to find; and if you do find it, "it doesn't pay to put it in." Besides it may not be the part you suspect that is causing the trouble. It could be the whole flugelpump. To find out for sure, you can put in a new flugelpump. If the device still doesn't work, then you know that it's something other than the flugelpump that's causing the trouble, but it "doesn't pay" to pull out the new flugelpump and put back the old one. It may be just a valve that you cannot get because "they're out of them right now."

There is a place on Myrtle Avenue which carries valves. You can take the flugelpump to the valve, but the valve and the man who can put in the valve are never in the same building at the same time.

"We've got the valve, but the mechanic is out."

"Where's the boss?"
"He's out with the mechanic."

∽ ∽

When we moved into our house we received a blender in the mail by mistake. Without opening the box, we mailed it back to the company. In two weeks it was back again with a note: "We have repaired your blender." There was a small charge of $7.80 for labor and a postage charge of $1.25. We did not pay. We stuck the thing, sealed up in its box, in the back of a closet, and neither the blender nor the company has given us any more trouble.

∽ ∽

We have our TV set in our bedroom. It has a remote-control channel changer which, as almost anybody these days can tell you, is a great conveniece for people who, like me, watch TV from bed at night. This convenience, however, works only if I inconveniently get out of bed and walk slowly, changer in hand, to within an inch of the bloodshot eye in the upper-right-hand corner of the set. To perform this operation without falling over furniture, I must first turn on the three-way lamp next to the bed. Like most three-way lamps ours promises bright/brighter/brightest, but delivers only

127

one, of its own choosing. The switch clicks three times; the bulb goes just On or Off. I paid for three ways: I'm gonna get three ways. I unscrew the bulb and shake it next to my ear. How long do you shake a bulb? Until it stops twingling inside, they say. Done. Screw it back into the socket. Now it doesn't work at all. Is it dead? There is only one way to find out.

I try it in another lamp, just a plain old-fashioned one-way lamp. It doesn't light. Maybe it's the socket of test lamp number-two and not the bulb of lamp number-one at all. It may even be the outlet in the wall. I move two bureaus in the dark to find an outlet. I locate a third lamp in another room and try it on the fresh outlet. It works on the third lamp but not on the second lamp. I get a ladder, remove a lighted bulb from the ceiling fixture and insert my dead bulb. It works. I reinsert the bulb I just took out. Now it doesn't light. Maybe I used the dead bulb instead of the good bulb. While I am up there swinging from the chandelier, my wife walks in.

"What are you doing up there?"

"I'm changing the channel."

"While you're changing the channel, clean out the dead flies." I make my way down to the floor carrying dead bulbs and dead flies.

I finally settle for screwing a one-way bulb into the three-way socket. I flip the switch three times; the bulb lights once. I now return to operation remote control and make it just in time to catch the good-night "Sermonette" on the subject of "Positive Thinking."

I think positively, shut off the TV set and return to the great joy of my life—good music, to be provided by my hi-fi, AM/FM combination radio and record player.

It has buttons marked Tape-Head, Phono I, Phono II, Microphone, AM/FM, FM Multiplex, Auxiliary, Channel A, Channel B, Stereo, Stereo Reverse, Treble Left, Treble Right, Bass Left, Bass Right, Volume, Balance Left Only, Right Only, Normal, Low-Frequency Filter, High-Frequency Filter, Selector, Monitor, 78, RIAA, Old Col LP, Phono Equalizer, 50 Play 100, Signal Strength, Center Channel, Station Selector, Muting Control, On and Off.

In addition to all of my engineering responsibilities (which leave me very little time for listening to music), I have had to learn to handle a record properly, to keep the playing surfaces away from dust, heat, cold, humidity and people, as well as to use a pickup with a stylus weight of not more than two grams, or approximately $\frac{1}{16}$ of an ounce.

Most of the time I find it less taxing to tune in to some good FM station, one which takes proper care of its equipment and can keep the police and airplane calls down to a minimum.

By the way, both my machine and recordings are now "out." Tape cassettes are "in."

❦ ❦

TV has brought us back to the Dark Ages. We sit amongst shadows eating peanuts and drinking beer. The answer to "Good evening" is "Shhh!" At eleven P.M. the lights are turned on, everybody says "Hello" and goes home.

To refute the contention that television has done nothing to raise the moral level of American life, I should like to point out the areas in which the great, new medium has emphasized the virtues we all hold dear.

Since the industry is too modest to credit itself publicly for its achievements, I have taken it upon myself to indicate how subtly moral values *are* beamed via satellite onto the mind of the unsuspecting viewer.

Here is a partial list of virtues, and the words, situations or shows which promote those virtues:

1. Helpfulness:   "They went thataway."
2. Perseverance:  Special Request Repeat of Last Summer's Rerun of "Another Evening with Fred Astaire."
3. Obedience:     "Go and tell your mother to buy you this Idio-toy, now!"
4. Mercy:         "The video portion of this program has been temporarily interrupted."
5. Faith:         "We'll be seeing you at the same time at the same place next week."

6. Hospitality:     "Johnny Carson's Return Visit to Dean Martin on the Bob Hope Visits Dean Martin's Tribute to The Johnny Carson Show."

7. Candor:     "I'm a big star from Hollywood, and look at *my* armpit!"

8. Easing the Life of Shut-ins:     "Warden, may I stay up to watch TV tonight? My crime is being re-enacted."

9. Freedom of Speech:     "The opinions expressed on this program are not necessarily condoned by the management of this station" (or even understood by them).

10. The One-World Outlook:     "We have just received a bulletin of earth-shattering importance to all of mankind; but first, a word from our sponsor."

∽ ∾

There is a variety of ratings systems whose purpose it is to find out what the public prefers to watch on TV. Sponsors also conduct private polls to find out which people watch which show. Sponsors who sell soap are genuinely interested in finding an audience that needs soap—not a dirty audience, just one that is soap-conscious.

Following is a questionnaire compiled by Sponsacademy, an independent research organization, to determine whether you are the type sought after by TV sponsors. In other words, are you the Consummate Consumer?

1. Are you deep-inside, really-truly positive you're not offending?
2. Does candy melt in your hand?
3. Is your bra "living," or just hanging around?
4. Do you look like *this* in the morning?
5. Do your children skate on your waxed floors?
6. Do you believe that products which contain ingredients work four times faster in the stomachs of patients whose doctors recommend ingredients?

Commercial TV's centerfold girl is one who has dry skin, briar-patch legs, itchy scalp, tired blood, drab hair, brittle nails, flabby chins, dull eyes and wobbly dental plates. If you have any or all of these qualifications, or if you know of a lovely girl who has, pick up an entry blank at your local hospital.

∽ ∽

As for our children, there isn't an American home left without at least one kid sitting in the dark in front of the TV set for from three to six hours per day. Some haven't been out of the house in seven years. Larger and larger screens, larger and larger eyeglasses. His mother is glad he watches Westerns. At least he gets a little fresh air and sunshine.

You can't talk to a kid when he's in front of the set. However, if the man on the set talks to him, he answers him. "Yes. I'll go. I'll buy it. I'll send two box tops. P.O. Box 495, Ma! Write it down!" In the middle of the night he wakes you. "Did it come yet?"

There is a good possibility that tomorrow's children will be born with one eight-fingered hand for pushing buttons, and a second hand, with only two fingers, located somewhere near the head, for purposes of scratching it. There will not be much else to do. The generation after that, children will say: "It's not automatic; you have to push a button."

～ ～

Science has extended our years, but deprived us of time.

I have felt the time of my life ebbing away as I marked time not only in repair shops and in supermarkets, but in or at airports, service stations, buses, elevators, restaurants, banks, post offices, box offices, doctors' and dentists' offices, information desks, reservation desks, confirmation desks. All the more frustrating because I had rushed to get there to save time and because it is happening to me *now* at the height of the instamatic age. I don't want speed; I want time. I would like to take my time, but it is being taken from me. Help! I'm being robbed!

❧ ❧

Mama lived *with* time, but not *on* time or *for* time. She measured her days not by seconds, minutes or hours, but by the milestones and tombstones that marked the road of her life. "May God give us time; troubles will come by themselves." *What time* it happened seemed trivial to Mama as against what happened at the time. *When* seemed much less important than *to whom* and *how* she felt when "it" happened.

Her moments of truth were imprinted on the heart rather than on the calendar. They were not just happenings, but happinessings and unhappinessings, full of emotional as well as historical impact—holidays, disasters, births, deaths, miracles, narrow escapes—handed down, as the Bible was, by word of mouth.

Time had purpose, but not always the purpose of one's choice. Mama had prepared us. There is a time, she said, for weeping and a time for rejoicing, and for lighting memorial candles, a time for silence, for speaking, a time to come home and a time to leave home, a time for dying (and she would spit three times—poo, poo, poo), and "time a big boy like you should know better than to say 'Tomorrow I will go . . .' Only a fool says 'Tomorrow I will.' If God will live and be healthy, and Papa will be all right too, then we'll see."

Daylight Saving Time, she said, is like cutting off the end of a blanket and sewing it onto the other end to make it longer. After the summer you cut if off again and put it back where you cut it off to make it shorter. "Very smart."

All this playing around with time may have thrown us out of sync with eternity.

∽ ∽

Mama could tell the passing of time without looking at the clock. When the light of dawn arrived at her bedroom window (always a little late, since it had to climb over tall tenements to get there), it was time for waking and working. Light coming through the kitchen window meant that her children would soon be home from school for lunch. By early afternoon (darkness came early for us) the rays of the setting sun would briefly touch our front room, informing Mama that the day was over. Yet, for at least a half-hour she would defiantly not turn on the lights. "I got time."

∽ ∽

If Mama could feel intangibles like time, she certainly could feel tangibles like silk, wool or cotton. No labeling of fabrics was necessary. "They're gonna tell *me* what's silk? I'll tell *them*!" Then along came silklike, woollike, cottonlike fabrics, the better than natural, pure ersatz, genuine imitation, smoother than, stronger than, lighter than, wrinkle-proof, runproof, rainproof, stain-proof, weakening Grandma's moral fiber into an acceptance of synthetic fiber.

To confuse us even more, the label on a single garment may account for 40 percent Dacron, 40 percent cotton and 30 percent reconstituted tapioca pudding that adds up to a total content of 110 percent of which part must be dry-cleaned, another part rinsed, another part ironed, another part never ironed under penalty of the law.

What is not there to begin with can be sprayed on.

Gun-control legislation should be expanded to include spray-gun registration. The domestic fallout has become a serious menace. Every household today contains an arsenal of spray cans in the hands of trigger-happy Americans who believe that the family that sprays together stays together, even sticks together.

There are as many varieties of aerosol cans as there are shotguns. Hair spray, for example, comes in: Hard-to-Manage-Hair Spray, Normal-to-Manage-Hair Spray, Easy-to-Manage-Hair Spray, Very-Easy-to-Manage-Hair Spray, Spray Hair Coloring,

Spray Hair-Coloring Remover, Spray Hair Remover, Spray Hair-Remover Remover.

When spray barbecue flame-starter and spray underarm deodorant are shot out of identical weapons, there are bound to be accidental injuries, like barbecued armpits, or perhaps even a living Venus de Milo?

∽∽

Somewhat akin to the ancient doctrine of original sin is the contemporary doctrine of original ugly, which teaches that we are all as "ugly as sin" and are doomed to become even more so, save for the intercession of the cosmetologists, the self-anointed high priests and priestesses of synthetic beauty.

Nature's brutal mistreatment of us has to be remedied by the constant application of balms, salves, lotions, potions, liniments, unguents, emollients, eyewashes, plasters, restoratives, astringents and jellies, all of which are intended to give us that "natural" look.

A perplexed, young college man told me, "It's a funny thing. Try to seduce a girl and she may cry a little. Touch her hairdo and she'll scream." This young man obviously had no idea how much care had gone into that incredibly natural free fall of waist-length hair.

It is conceivable that in the not-too-distant future

a man will be able to have a marriage legally annulled on the grounds of deceptive packaging.

As the bride comes down the aisle in her fiberglass gown, plastic shoes and Lucite tiara, she is indeed a "living doll." On the honeymoon, however, as she prepares to be a wife, she removes her wig, her deep-blue contact lenses, her cellophane eyelashes, her stick-on exotic fingernails and her foam-rubber bust. The young groom may not only wonder *who* she is, but *where* she is. She has gone from disposable to invisible before his very eyes.

෴

The nose forgery, while it may deliver instant beauty and all of its fringe benefits, including marriage, can also impose all the penalties of complicity in a conspiracy: fear of public detection, distrust of one's confederates and inviolate secrecy.

To keep the unnatural nose an act of God rather than a pact of man, it is sometimes necessary to retroactively fix the nose of the girl's mother so that the girl's nose makes some sense. Fathers' noses may run as crooked as they like. Grandmas' noses have to be watched. Grandpas are beyond remedy. If in doubt, he should not be invited to the wedding. Brothers and sisters should keep their old noses. This makes the girl even more strikingly beautiful by comparison, chosen to live out the Cinderella syndrome.

The real danger of betrayal lies not in the past but in the future. The girl's firstborn, completely unaware of the plot on his genes, may burst upon the world with a nasal flashback that can shake the integrity of an entire dynasty, except that the girl's side has already prepared itself for such a calamity with an unbreakable alibi: "That's from his side of the family." If the kid's father doesn't swallow that, he can be comforted with the old cliché: "On a boy it doesn't matter."

∽ ∽

I wonder if the synthetic world we are bequeathing to our children may not be at least partly responsible for sending them off on drug trips, in search of lost senses.

Too many kids seem to have decided that they cannot achieve "lightness of extremities," "floating on air," "a quickened heartbeat," "joyous dreams," "euphoria," "a tingling sensation," "a feeling of peace," "intensified colors" and "keener hearing," without the aid of junk, LSD, morphine, goofballs, snow, speed or ups. At the peak of our scientific sophistication they have returned to primitive witchcraft: bloodletting, skin-pricking, smoking of weeds, inhaling of magical vapors.

Children are born quivering bundles of sensation, exquisitely turned on. Yet in the prime of their youth they are pumping artificial ecstacy into their bloodstreams. Are overdoses of drugs caused by underdoses of the joy of living?

Ecstacy begins at home. In the hands of a talented food pusher, meatballs can be as stimulating as goofballs. If enough of them are eaten late enough at night, they will spark dreams. I know a bit about dreams but I am an expert on heartburn. It is not a disease; it is a breathtaking experience. Despite much malicious propaganda, it is regarded by those of us who have been on intimate terms with it as a major source of unquenchable sense memories. Home is where the heart burns. Unless you can recall that middle of the night when the gush of cold seltzer hit the flame in your gut, you can lay no claim to familiarity with psychedelic phenomena.

A cold flat can be converted into a warm home with a pot of hot soup. I am a survivor of Mama's molten-lava treatment. One spoonful of her soup and I became a dragon, puffing smoke, some of it through my ears. I could feel the hot fluid mainlining it through my blood vessels.

If I ever made the mistake of trying to put out the fire by swallowing cold water, I found myself percolating. Between snorts and coughs I would express admiration: "It's great [puff], Ma [puff]. Thanks [puff], Ma."

To a kid coming home from school, there is no warmer reception than soup vapor spelling out

140

"Welcome home!" Frozen foods can only spell "Come back later."

I am not naive enough to think that soup or meatballs is a cure-all for modern ills. I cite them only as symbols of the relationship between child and home.

∽∽

And what about us elders who were brought up with the old values? Why is there so little euphoria in our crowd? We, too, have lost our senses. We are so wound up in our daily pursuit of a luxurious tomorrow that we cannot sleep tonight. We need pills to unwind us. We say we want to sleep, but it may be amnesia we're after. Swallow an "off" button and drop off. It's a great life if you don't waken.

The drug companies are more than willing to anesthetize us. They are the legal pushers.

"Are you suffering from 'simple nervous tension' "? Here on the counter at your fingertips lies instant tranquility. Try Dozo, Snoozo, Snoro, Dreamo, Nappo, Yawno, Zombo or Damitol. In the morning you may need an "on" pill. Try Revivo, Returno, Socko, Adrenalo or Combaco. Take the wrong pill and you may be brilliant all night and stupid all day.

In our pursuit of instant happiness we got hooked on television, booze, money, automation, cars, credit cards, synthetics, computers which, instead of inducing the hoped-for euphoria, have produced only the side effects of addiction: impaired judgment, panic, outbursts of temper, nightmares, paranoia and delusions of grandeur. This is the grim world of the brothers happy.

Now may be the time to defrost the ideas and ideals of early America, to try to recapture those moments in our history when our senses were bursting with national pride. Perhaps we should retrace our steps to find out when, where and, most important, *why* we lost our joyous dreams. . . .

∽ ∽

Many of our young are, in fact, going back to the past, to the earth, to working with their hands, to mastering ancient crafts, to small shops and street-vending—just like the men in Mama's life. They give birth naturally, nurse their babies and carry them on their backs. They bake bread, eat organic foods and, like Grandma, have long lists of edibles that are kosher or not kosher according to the new ecological rules. They are nostalgic for a past they never knew, back somewhere between the Fall and the fallout, when body and soul were one, innocent and uncontaminated.

∽ ∽

11

*In Marriage . . .*

*. . . as in everything else, it is getting harder to get things repaired or even to get replacements for the parts that have worn out. "Get a new one." Couples now would rather switch than fight. That's the new happy ending.*

∽ ∽

It is true that people are still marrying for better or for worse, for richer or for poorer, but not for long. Funny thing. Lots of people can't live without each other—until they get married; then they can. (United we stand; but separated we can stand it even better.) The trend indicates that marrying the one you love is much easier than loving the one you married and that constancy in marriage is much harder than constantly getting married.

"I do" and "Adieu" are running neck and neck.

Love and marriage no longer seem to go together like a horse and carriage, or is it that the age of the horse and carriage was a better age for marriage? Or is it that horses, carriages and marriages have all become obsolete?

For many of our young, wedlock seems to be on the way out. They are conscientious objectors to all locks. They are afraid that even a simple gold wedding band may cut off their circulation.

∽ ∽

Whatever the causes may be, one giant paradox confronts us: since people started to marry for love and love alone, as free men should (not like Mama and Papa), and started to settle their differences reasonably, as free men should (not like Mama and Papa), the rate of broken marriages has accelerated. Even the broken marriages are not doing well, and the partners often have to get together again.

It is no longer death but life that parts. The split-level marriage (living in one place and loving in another) is becoming not only more common but more commonly accepted. It is not easy to cast stones at people who are always on the move between bed and board. All attachments (romantic as well as electronic) now come with a long extension cord that can be plugged in anywhere. Everybody's gone AWOL—Away on Love. The bluebird of happiness lives away from home. There have been several attempts (all failures) to compile a *Who's Whose in America*. Everybody seems to be making house calls but doctors. Perhaps it's only a liberal interpretation of the injunction "Love thy neighbor."

∾ ∾

One does not have to read statistics to realize that the current state of marriage is not very good. What we may presently have is not a marital union but a loose confederacy of males and females pronounced (and just as often mispronounced) husband and wife. One has but to listen to the woeful tales of the lawful wedded about their awful spouses:

"I can't prove he's been unfaithful, but I doubt that he's the father of my child."

*

"I know she's incompatible, although I've never actually caught her at it."

*

"It was driving me crazy. I didn't know where he spent his evenings. One night I went home and there he was."

*

147

"I knew he couldn't be trusted. He has gone back to his wife."

*

"I see so little of him, I feel like I took his name in vain."

❦ ❦

It was hard to tell whether our papas and mamas were happily married. The subject was not open for discussion, certainly not with their children.

"Are you happy, Ma?"

"I got nothing else to think about?"

Nobody had ever told Mama that marriage was supposed to make her happy; certainly Papa hadn't. Nobody had promised *him* happiness either. Mature people prayed for good health, good fortune and an honorable old age. A husband was supposed to make a living and a wife was supposed to make a life of it. Only children talked of happiness; they still believed in fairy tales. Human beings, the old folks said, don't live happily forever after—most of the time not even during. So it was wise in marriage and in everything else to expect the worst. Then if it turned out to be only worse, it still wasn't too bad. Marriage was one of those things you were supposed to save for your old age, happy or not.

To Mama love was not passion, or infatuation or compatibility. She had given birth to ten kids without any of those. "Love," said Mama after many years of marriage, "is what you have been through with someone."

Love was made up of satisfaction ("Eight kids, thank God, is plenty"); sharing ("If he can take it, I can take it"); optimism ("Worse it couldn't get!"); and friendship, not in the style of Romeo and Juliet, but more like Damon and Pythias.

❦ ❦

It would seem that our constant exposure to marital quarrels might have made us prematurely cynical. On the contrary, our early combat training taught us to bring our "as you like it" into focus with "like it is," not on the subject of marriage alone but on human partnerships in general.

We came to realize that every man and woman has something to say in his own defense; that there are not two sides to an argument, but dozens; that one of the reasons God said "Thou Shalt Not Kill" was that you might not yet have heard all sides of the story; that in human relations there is no perfect and final answer; that some ideas may never be happily wedded to others; that the dialogue, whispered or shouted, is eternal; and that the seeking of the answer is the answer.

We had absorbed a mature point of view: there's nothing wrong with marriage; it's just the living together afterward that's murder.

〜〜

*A Few Thoughts for Newly Married Couples Gathered from Successful Practitioners:*

The only person who listens to both sides of a husband-and-wife argument is the woman in the next apartment.

You can never tell until you're married, and then, even if you can, you shouldn't.

When you think your marriage has gone down for the third time, just remember maybe you counted wrong.

There are three types of happily married couples: the ones who make things happen; the ones who watch things happen; and the ones who don't know what's happening.

〜〜

12

# What Every Boy
# Should Know . . .

## ... *but I still don't.*

❧ ❧

Not only do the young today know more about sex than I knew when I was their age; they know more about it at their age now than I know at my age now.

My parents never heard of Freud. In our building there was one Fried, one Freund and two Friedmans. But no Freud.

Mama used one four-letter word. It was designed as a contraceptive against four-letter deeds. The word was *"don't."* A clean mind in a clean body: for the mind, *"don't"*; for the body, soap.

"It's better if you wait," we were told.

We were used to waiting. We waited for Papa to sit at the table before we ate, for the lighting of the Sabbath candles, for new shoes, for steam heat, for a job, for money, for marriage. "Save it for your wife," they told me. I was already old enough to know what a wife was, but I still didn't know what "it" was.

153

A girl's plea to her mother that "I'm not a baby anymore" brought an answer like "That's why I want you home by nine o'clock."

Mamas generally warned their daughters to: "Just say 'No,' because before you can say 'Look here, I'd like you to know that I am not that kind of a girl,' you may already be one."

∾ ∾

The "early-to-bed" movement seems to be recruiting hosts of devout adherents. The sexperts recommend teen-age relations to the full on the grounds that it is natural and honest and, therefore, moral. To deny this natural urge, they say, is an act of hypocrisy that will leave the adolescent a mass of inhibitions. All that is required of the followers of this philosophy is sincerity and one partner at a time. One at a time is love. Two is promiscuous. With three it's sexual independence and, beyond that, research. All this sexual activity is known as playing it cool.

∾ ∾

Our young, ready or not, are driven by the need to prove themselves sexually liberated. There are new tests to be passed every day, and there is no Graduation Day. The requirements of high frequency may instigate a loveless preoccupation with satisfying an obligation not so much to one's own body as to the bodies of more committed sextavists. It takes courage for a Daughter of the Sexual Revolution to say, "Let me off this streetcar named Desire. I don't care to go to the last stop. Please!"

～ ～

Exhibition has replaced inhibition. Just when I got used to the fresh-air propagation of cats and dogs, the kids took over. The cats and dogs are now standing around watching the kids. Only heaven knows what the dumb animals will learn from the smart kids. Just wait till the animals find out that the kids don't even have a license.

～ ～

The movies provide visual aids. Modern camera technique utilizes the zoom lens which gives a couple the kind of physical that would take six days at the Mayo Clinic. The camera goes where even the X-ray fears to tread—into nostrils, eyeballs, ear canals. "Lovers" don't necessarily love each other but they do knead each other badly.

Most of what I see on the movie screen strikes me not as intended "FOR MATURE AUDIENCES ONLY," but for immature audiences only. Box-office seduction of the emotionally deprived. Group voyeurism at $4.50 per hour.

Nudity onstage is not necessarily obscene. Some nudes reveal nothing but flesh; others, the soul of a human being. I am sorry for those who are being sold soul-free skin and bones as the whole human being. They are being cheated. Mama would have said simply: "Don't buy by him."

My sex education was far from ideal. It was typical of its time. Waiting was never easy. (The urge was often urgent.) Yet, I sometimes wonder whether it wasn't easier for us to wait than to have to prove our maturity upon demand. Instant sex like instant coffee may not necessarily be the best.

"Make love, not war" is not a peace slogan but a sex slogan. If making love is all there is to love, then streetwalkers should be revered and remembered tenderly on St. Valentine's Day. If the act of lovemaking rather than the sanctity of loving is to be the summum bonum of our civilization, gynecologists should be our Doctors of Divinity.

Man is as much in need of a course in remedial love as in remedial sex. He has yet to bring his ethical urge up to the level of his sexual urge. Right now passion is running ahead of compassion.

∽ ∽

Most people agree that children should be told the facts of life. What we disagree on are the facts.

It is easy to draw a diagram and indicate where the little sperm goes to keep its rendezvous with the little egg, but are these *all* the facts?

If we are going to teach a child about the nature of human life, it is essential that from the minute he begins to "wonder" he be introduced bit by bit to the wonder of life and of love. Unless we can transmit to the child an attitude of reverence, we are merely discussing plumbing.

The offering of one's self, the supreme act of cherished privacy shared in love, can be so easily degraded. The best we can give our teen-agers is a philosophy that will help them to handle their biological desires with dignity, a philosophy which teaches that the human body is a private treasure and not a public playground.

A youngster will exercise self-restraint if he has been taught to approach sex with awe. He will understand genuine love when he realizes that the mysterious force which moves him to love is the same force that moves the universe. This force has many names: God, Nature, Omnipotence, Omniscience, Truth, Mind, Spirit, Supreme Being, Essence, Life. . . .

∽ ∾

When my daughter started to date we talked about being beautiful. I suggested to her that the truly "beautiful people" are not necessarily in the jet set, but in the soul set. I even suggested several time-tested beauty hints:

*For attractive lips, speak words of kindness.*

*For lovely eyes, seek out the good in people.*

*For a slim figure, share your food with the hungry.*

*For beautiful hair, let a child run his fingers through it once a day.*

*For poise, walk with the knowledge that you will never walk alone.*

And one of these days some guy just might say, "Gee, baby, you're beautiful." He might even want to marry you.

∽ ∽

# *Epilogue*

While all the previous pages would indicate that I am a traditionalist, I do not believe that the past was always better than the present. I know only that the future had better be better than the present. (You can say that again, Sam.)

I know that we cannot turn the clock back to a simpler, gentler age, but we can try to move ahead in time to a simpler, gentler age.

The pursuit of happiness has obviously failed. I don't believe we shall ever be happy until we turn to the pursuit of truth, compassion, equality, love and justice and insist that all our institutions—our schools, our homes, our churches, our industries, our technology, our government—reflect the sanctity of human life.

Even humor is not exempt from the exhortation to love one's neighbor as one's self.

Manslaughter is but an apostrophe removed from man's laughter.

I have tried to laugh *with*, never *at*. I hope you have laughed along with me.

*Sam*

# LOOK FOR THESE GREAT POCKET ⚓ BOOK BESTSELLERS AT YOUR FAVORITE BOOKSTORE

**THE PIRATE** • Harold Robbins

**YOU CAN SAY THAT AGAIN, SAM!** • Sam Levenson

**THE BEST** • Peter Passell & Leonard Ross

**CROCKERY COOKING** • Paula Franklin

**SHARP PRACTICE** • John Farris

**JUDY GARLAND** • Anne Edwards

**SPY STORY** • Len Deighton

**HARLEQUIN** • Morris West

**THE SILVER BEARS** • Paul E. Erdman

**FORBIDDEN FLOWERS:**
**More Women's Sexual Fantasies** • Nancy Friday

**MURDER ON THE ORIENT EXPRESS** • Agatha Christie

**THE JOY OF SEX** • Alex Comfort

**RETURN JOURNEY** • R. F. Delderfield

**THE TEACHINGS OF DON JUAN** • Carlos Castaneda

**JOURNEY TO IXTLAN** • Carlos Castaneda

**A SEPARATE REALITY** • Carlos Castaneda

**TEN LITTLE INDIANS** • Agatha Christie

**BABY AND CHILD CARE** • Dr. Benjamin Spock

**BODY LANGUAGE** • Julius Fast

**THE MERRIAM-WEBSTER DICTIONARY**
(Newly Revised)